Drugs and Schoolchildren

Drugs and Schoolchildren

R. S. P. Wiener, Ph.D.

Longman

Longman Group Limited
London
Associated companies, branches and representatives
throughout the world

First published 1970

SBN 582 50704 9

This book is an adaptation of a Ph.D. thesis
'Drug taking among school children'
University of London 1969.

Set in 11pt. Garamond and Printed in Great Britain by
The Camelot Press Ltd., London and Southampton

To M

Contents

Acknowledgements

This book would never have been written without the never-ending assistance I received from Mrs Hamilton.

I also wish to particularly thank Dr A. N. Oppenheim who was my supervisor for the major part of the research and Dr G. Edwards for his helpful and relevant criticisms.

My gratitude also goes to John Bynner of Government Social Survey and Miss Joy Mott of the Home Office Research Unit who both gave me the benefit of their experience in related fields of research.

Thanks are also due to Mrs Stone, Miss Campling, Brenda Jordan, Jane Taylor and Mrs Joan Peake who all helped to prepare various drafts of this manuscript.

I am greatly indebted to the probation officers, educational authorities and headmasters who cooperated in this research. I would also like to extend my gratitude to the 1,093 school children who gave up an hour of their schooling to complete the questionnaires.

Finally I would like to thank the Home Office who supplied a grant for the larger part of this research.

PART ONE

The Problem and the Background to the Hypotheses

1 Introduction

It is essential at the outset, before proceeding to discuss the reasons for this study, to spend some time first, in defining what one means by the term 'drugs', secondly, in providing a brief description of each of the most commonly used drugs, how they are taken, by whom and with what effects, and thirdly, in explaining some of the terms frequently used in the field. These three points will be considered in particular reference to the English situation.

DEFINITION OF 'DRUGS'

A 'drug' is defined by the *Concise Oxford Dictionary* as an 'original simple medicinal substance, organic or inorganic, used alone or as an ingredient'. The modern colloquial use of the term, however, refers to the usage of drugs in a non-medical setting. In keeping with this, Laurie (137:11)[1] defines the term 'drug' as; 'any chemical substance that alters mood, perception or consciousness and is misused, to the apparent detriment of society'. This is the definition that will be used in this book.

The following discussion on drugs is meant to serve simply as an introduction to the subject. The discussion does not include a comprehensive and critical review of the literature relevant to each group of drugs.[2] The discussion merely presents some of the available facts about each of the drugs and some of the opinions as to their good and bad effects. As the subsequent review will show, the literature consists, to a large extent, of expressed

---

[1] The first number in the bracket refers to the bibliography and subsequent numbers refer to the page in the original text from which the quote is taken.

[2] Reviews of the literature on drugs are available elsewhere. See, for example, Sir Aubrey Lewis's review of the cannabis literature in Appendix 1 of the *Wootton Report* (109).

opinions with comparatively few, well carried out, objective studies to either prove or disprove them.

USAGE AND EFFECTS

The main groups of drugs which are misused by young people and which are therefore the concern of this book are: the opiates (in particular heroin), cannabis, hallucinogenic drugs (in particular LSD), amphetamines, barbiturates and finally amphetamine and barbiturate combinations. Chein *et al.* (45:342–3) label the amphetamines, cannabis and the hallucinogens as 'psychic modifiers' because of their effect on mood, ideation, affect, feeling, anxiety, pain or tension and points out that they can be either used in distressing organic diseases or they can be used for their effects on the psychic organisation itself.

An important point to realise is that societal attitudes towards specific drugs alter greatly over time, as do the attitudes of groups within societies. To quote Chein *et al.* (45:337): 'These drugs [opiates and cannabis] have not always been regarded ... [as] inherently dangerous, even poisonous substances ... on the other hand, not only alcohol but even coffee and tobacco have been prescribed as harmful and undesirable substances.'

As the following discussion will show, and as a London School of Economics study (16) revealed, not only are there inter-drug differences in alleged effect but there are also intra-drug differences due to changes, in the person taking the drug, in mood, in the setting, etc. This is a reason for the necessity of considering social factors when discussing drug abuse.

Pep pills

Nearly all the drugs called 'pep pills' consist of a preparation of amphetamine, either by itself or in combination with another drug, usually a barbiturate. There are, according to Connell (56:234), more than fifty of these preparations on the market at the present time. These include, say Leech and Jordan (139:5–6), dexamphetamine (dexedrine), known among teenagers as 'dexies', methylamphetamine or methedrine known as 'meth', benzedrine known as 'bennies' and drinamyl known as 'purple hearts'. The latter is an amphetamine/barbiturate combination.

The first pep pill to be synthesised was benzedrine, in the United States in 1927 (Leech and Jordan: 139:26). Since then, Connell (56:234–7) claims, they have been used clinically in a number of conditions—narcolepsy, Parkinsonism, epilepsy, barbiturate poisoning, drug addiction and alcoholism, psychopathic states, behaviour disorders in children, enuresis, obesity, depression and abreactive treatment. The fact that they are frequently used in general medicine also is shown by the fact that in 1965 3·8 million prescriptions for amphetamines alone were issued by the National Health Service (Leech and Jordan: 139:29).

The peripheral effects of the drug are, according to Connell (56:234),

> sympathomimetic and include an increase in blood pressure, dilation of the pupils, relaxation of the smooth muscle of the gastro-intestinal tract, urinary bladder and bronchioles and the secretion of thick saliva . . . as well as these sympathomimetic effects, various stimulating effects on the central nervous system were shown to occur, such as arousal, wakefulness, euphoria, lessening of fatigue and increased energy and self-confidence.

These latter reasons are part of the explanation why these drugs are taken illicitly. One of the first signs that this was occurring in a large way was Anne Sharpley's articles in the *Evening Standard* (183) in 1964, about the prevalence of pill taking in the Soho district of London. That such a problem exists and continues to do so is shown by the fact that between the end of 1964 and the beginning of 1966 there were 1600 prosecutions and 1500 convictions for unauthorised possession of amphetamines, most of them in London (Leech and Jordan 139:29). The pep pills used illegally, come from three main sources: '(1) illicit imports from overseas; (2) thefts from manufacturers . . . and from chemists' shops; (3) over-prescription by doctors, and forged prescriptions' (Leech and Jordan 139:28).

Scott and Willcox (180:13) report that among the other reasons given for the illegal use of pep pills is the claim that taking them 'peps you up . . . makes you feel awake . . . gives you vitality . . . you can talk like anyone else . . . you don't care what's said about you . . . you can stay awake all weekend'. In more general terms Connell (56:238) says that abuse comes when people wish to experience the psychological effects of the drug, namely the euphoria and tendency to loquaciousness and diminution of inhibitions.

Whereas many teenagers start and continue to take only one or two pills at a time a number move on to using them in greater quantities. Bestic (17:40) records one youngster as saying: 'At first I only took three for a try out. All of a sudden I was feeling better than I've ever felt in my life. So I took more and more, thinking I'd get a bigger and better kick. But it didn't work that way. Soon I was taking them more or less to keep normal. I had to take them.' As Leech and Jordan (139:28) explain:

> The user will find that in order to maintain the effect of the pill he needs to increase the dose . . . after a large dose physical exertion may be much increased but when it has worn off there is a greater fatigue and depression than before and a longer period of rest is required. In misuse situations the misuser keeps taking more of the drug in an endeavour to avoid this 'come down' feeling of greater fatigue and greater depression.

This can lead, says Connell (54:11), to (1) overactivity leading to social consequences, (2) production of psychotic illness of a 'schizophrenic type', (3) shock and collapse, (4) risk of suicide, and (5) the production of addiction and habituation.

There is some doubt as to whether pep pills can produce any degree of physical dependence.[1] The World Health Organisation (213), while stating that tolerance and a degree of psychic[2] dependence upon the drug will occur, say that there is a general absence of physical dependence. This view is supported by Eddy and Isbell (67:730) and by Knapp (131:426). However, Bell and Trethowan (14:495) report that they have treated cases of amphetamine dependence, and Hawks et al. (100) report a study of seventy-four regular users of methylamphetamine all of whom on average had been using the drug continuously for the past nineteen months.

The evidence seems to suggest that while a considerable number of pep pill takers stay as occasional users, some develop a degree of psychic dependence upon the drug and because of the tolerance effect take ever increasing amounts. Do many amphetamine-takers go a step further and progress to other drugs? This is impossible to say with any certainty, though Bewley (19:809) in a study of thirty-three heroin addicts found twelve had taken pep pills previously, while Willis (208:225) found that 95 per cent of a sample of heroin addicts had taken amphetamines previously. What one cannot say is what proportion of amphetamine takers

---

[1] See p. 16 for discussion of drug terminology.

[2] Psychic is used in this context to mean 'pyschological'.

who do move on, this represents. As will be suggested later, this is likely to be a very small number.

Barbiturates

Barbiturates are often wrongly classified together with the amphetamines as 'pills'. Even though it might well be the case that these drugs are used on an irregular basis in the same kind of places and by the same groups of young people it is important to differentiate between them as they have completely different psychopharmacological actions. Whereas the amphetamines are central nervous stimulants the barbiturates act as depressants over (182:105) 'a wide range of cellular functions in many vital organ systems'. Similarly the effects of barbiturates are different from those described above for the amphetamines. 'Both the acute and chronic effects of mild barbiturate intoxication resemble those of intoxication with alcohol. The intoxicated individual shows a general sluggishness, difficulty in thinking, slowness of speech and comprehension, poor memory, faulty judgment, narrowed range of attention, emotional lability and exaggeration of basic personality traits' (120:296). It is possible to become addicted to barbiturates.

One should point out that barbiturates do not seem to be misused by young people to anywhere near the same extent as the amphetamines.

Cannabis

According to Chein et al. (45:343) the cannabis drugs, which have been known since 2737 B.C. 'are prepared from the flowering tops, leaves, seeds and stems of the hemp plant, "cannabis saliva" '. Andrews et al. (2:vii) say marijuana refers to the preparation made from the dried flowers of the female plant, while hashish is made from the resin with which the flowers are coated, coming off in the form of a golden powder when the plants are shaken. In The Book of Grass (2) over ninety-three names are given for this drug. Some of the more common, according to Fort (81:138), are marijuana, hashish, dagga, kif and ganga. As Wilson and Linken (209) point out, there are likely to be considerable differences in the content of the pharmacologically active agent in plants collected and prepared from different geographical areas. According to them the effect of cannabis appears to be caused by the stereoisomin, delta THC.

The effects of smoking cannabis, according to Winick (211:22),

Bᴅs

often occur in three stages, with an initial exhilaration, a peak midpoint and then a period of coming out. Specific effects are speaking freely, daydreaming, diminution of inhibitions and a pleasurable relaxation. Up to twenty-five minutes after starting a reefer (a cannabis cigarette) there is a feeling of anxiety and restlessness. This gives way to calmness and pleasant sensations, though Wilson and Linken (209) say that the novice 'after two or three puffs . . . invariably . . . becomes nauseated and dizzy after the first few inhalations and may vomit'. Winick (211:22) continues, that the effects for the more experienced user are that his body feels light and laughter is easy. Things seem to be happening very rapidly, perceptions become confused and memory usually deteriorates. This drug is not an aphrodisiac but is said to improve potency which may be because of the distortions of time which makes a period of sexual contact seem longer. Trocchi (194:95) goes even further on this point and says: 'Marijuana . . . provokes a more sensual (or aesthetic) kind of concentration, a detached articulation of minute areas, an ability to adopt play postures. What can be more relevant in the act of love?' In the cannabis/hallucinogenic participant observation study (see p. 47), members of the group did in fact use cannabis as an aphrodisiac. Winick (211:23) concludes that the speaker often confuses his rush of words and assumes that they are exceptionally clear. The response in our culture to the smoking of the drug tends to be passive, yet this passivity is not a universal response within Western society. A social worker (36) at a café in London which has a predominantly working-class, semicriminal membership reports incidents where members while 'high' on cannabis started fights. It appears likely therefore that both the surroundings within which the drug is taken and the personality of the user play a part in determining its effects. Because of the type of effects that cannabis gives, it is, report Chein *et al.* (45:345), used most often in a group setting.

There is much disagreement as to whether cannabis usage is harmful in either the short of the long term. As regards its short-term ill effects Scher (177:541) says cannabis enhances whatever tendencies are already present in the individual. Weil, Zinberg and Nelson in what is probably the first proper controlled test on marijuana concluded that (202:1241–2):

Marijuana naïve persons do demonstrate impaired performance on simple intellectual and psychomotor tests after smoking marijuana; the impairment is dose-related in some cases . . . regular users of marijuana do get high after smoking marijuana in a neutral setting but do not show the same degree of impairment of performance on the tests as do naïve subjects. In some cases, their performance even appears to improve slightly after smoking marijuana.

Isbell and White (119:564) say that toxic psychoses may occur in susceptible individuals. One cannabis user described to the experimenter how she had had a psychotic episode after smoking and eating a large quantity of cannabis. As regards long-term ill effects, a heroin addict, in describing his previous use of cannabis, which he said he had smoked every day for eighteen months, claimed that after a while his personality had peeled off like a large layer of onions so that every twenty minutes or so he 'flipped' over. Wilson and Linken (209) claim that a 'number of chronic (cannabis) smokers have been encountered in their late teens who find great difficulty in breaking the habit'. This is supported by Davies (62:5). Wilson and Linken (209) go on to say that 'these chronic smokers state their intellectual capacity is disturbed, constructive work is impossible and relationships to people and the environment altered . . . these people seem to suffer from some degree of psychic dependence coupled with a requirement for fairly high doses of the drug'.

On the other hand the World Health Organisation (213) point out that though there can be psychic dependence on the drug there is no evidence of any physical dependence. Supporting evidence for this comes from the New York Mayor's Report (200), Leech and Jordan (139:39) and Fort (81:138). Scher (177:541) says no functions are adversely effected while the New York Report (200) claimed that cannabis did not result in reactions alien to the personality.

Murphy (158:21) in a review of the literature in 1963 says:

Both in the complexity of its effects and in more specific characteristics, cannabis is much closer to alcohol than to the opiates or to cocaine. Like alcohol, it appears to have no deleterious effects on the moderate user . . . as with alcohol, single doses, given to naïve, unstable subjects can produce an acute confusion, perhaps with violence, while the long-term use of heavy doses can probably lead to partial dementia . . . it is clear that the free availability of cannabis can be harmful but it is not clear that this is more harmful than the free availability of alcohol.

Edwards (70:230), in a more recent look at the divergent views, says that

> the evidence as to whether marijuana can lead to brain damage, personality deterioration or chronic psychotic illness has also led to considerable debate but it seems fair to say that informed medical opinion is moving towards the view that there is no convincing evidence that deleterious long-term effects are produced by marijuana.

He does, however, say that in some cases there can be acute marijuana intoxication. Wilson and Linken (209), while pointing out the dangers of cannabis use above, do say that those who turn into chronic smokers are only a minority of the cannabis users.

Therefore the general effects of cannabis used moderately do not now appear to be particularly harmful. In fact Chein *et al.* (45:345) go on to say that cannabis is used in our society 'to attain an experience which, far from renouncing the active life in favour of a contemplative, ascetic ideal, affirms the pleasures of sex, music, food, laughter and human companionship'.

A more serious charge often levelled against cannabis usage is that it tends to lead to heroin. Willis (208:224) says that 'the regular user of marijuana is statistically more likely to encounter heroin users than a non-marijuana user. This increases his exposure to heroin, i.e. he encounters the habit by association.' Among the figures available to support these contentions are studies of addicts by Bewley (19) and Garmany (85), where in both cases over 50 per cent of the addicts had previously used cannabis. However, 100 per cent of them had probably smoked cigarettes. Obviously, therefore, not all cigarette smokers or all cannabis smokers become heroin addicts. The important question is, what percentage of cannabis users do? This is unknown but it does not appear to be very high for the Wootton report (109: para. 36) comments that guesses by witnesses put the number of cannabis users as between 30,000 and 300,000 while only 1796 addicts had signed on at treatment centres by July 1968 (110).

Hallucinogenics

Hallucinogenic drugs, often referred to as psychedelic or psychomimetic drugs, have been defined by Metzner quoted in Barrigar (9:394) as substances that produce changes in thought, perception, mood and, sometimes, in posture, occurring alone or in concert, without causing either major disturbances of the autonomic system or addictive craving and although, with overdosage, disorientation memory disturbance, stupor and even narcosis may occur, these reactions are not characteristic.

Some of the drugs classified in this group are: LSD, mescaline, psilocybin, morning glory seeds, DET (diethyl tryptamine), DMT (dimethyl kryptamine), and DPT (diephenyl tryptamine). According to Sandison (176:244), LSD is probably the most potent of the hallucinogenic group and is the most readily available and by far the most common in use in this country. This section will therefore concentrate on LSD to the exclusion of the other psychedelic drugs.

LSD was first synthesised in 1938 and its hallucinogenic properties were first discovered in 1943 (Sandison 176:244) by Dr Hofmann. An average dose of LSD is 100 micrograms (Cohen 50: 34). LSD is commonly taken as a liquid on sugar, or soaked into blotting paper or as blue pills (Sandison 176:246). A white pill reportedly from Czechoslovakia appears to be available on the London market (Participant observation study, see p. 47).

According to Cohen (50:35/38–9) the first effects of the drug will be felt, in the case of sensitive individuals, within fifteen minutes of taking it. The intensity of symptoms reaches a plateau after one and a half hours before terminating in six to twelve hours. The physical effects of the drug are, according to Cohen, enlargement of the pupil, a quicker and stronger knee jerk, unchanged blood pressure and pulse rates and only slight impairment of speech and other motor acts.

The psychological effects of the drug have often been recorded. They include, according to Cohen (50:42), the fact that separation between the self and the external world disappears, and a primeval thinking process intervenes; Sandison (176:247) adds, that in some cases there may be 'transcendental calm, of a sense of unity of all things, a detachment from the world and of oneness with the universe'.

These effects are by no means universally experienced. There are considerable differences reported both between individuals and between different drug-taking experiences of the same individual.

There is some doubt as to how LSD achieves its psychological effects. Klee (130:464–5), for example, says that LSD may work by both inhibiting stimuli, akin to sensory deprivation, yet also allowing a flooding of stimuli.

It was felt at first that LSD might be both clinically helpful and nonclinically dangerous to use because it appeared to produce a psychotic type state. Hence its early label as being a psycho-mimetic drug. However, as Cohen (50:90) points out, the LSD subject retains the saving knowledge that what is happpening is due to a drug and is temporary. In connection with other ill effects that might arise from the administration of the drug Cohen (50:212) estimates that one patient in every 2500 committed suicide after taking LSD. Sandison (176:245) says that the dangers of LSD are accentuated by the facts, first, that those who take it illicity are often emotionally disturbed and come from back-grounds which predispose them to emotional and psychotic disorder, and secondly, that there is a danger of accidental ingestion or deliberate secret administration of LSD occurring. This is possible because, not only is LSD extremely potent, but it is also odourless, tasteless and colourless.

It appears therefore that LSD can be very harmful if taken illegally by severely disturbed people. On the other hand hallu-cinogens do not cause physical dependence, though according to Eddy and Isbell (67:731), some degree of psychic dependence can occur. A high degree of tolerence to LSD develops rapidly and disappears rapidly. Cohen (50:37) reports that after three doses psychic effects disappear unless there has been an abstinence period of three days.

Louria (149:44) says that clinically some psychiatrists claim LSD is beneficial in the treatment of 'psychoses, psychoneuroses and frigidity . . . and it has been used as a substitute for analgesics on terminal cancer patients . . . there are some preliminary data suggesting that LSD may be beneficial in the treatment of alcoholics'. Its illegal use in this country, records Sandison (176: 246), is common among students and cases are likely to be encountered at all the universities and possibly at some colleges of further education, particularly art colleges. Sandison (176:245) goes on to say that its use in this country has been 'linked to the "Hippie movement", that group of non aggressive young people whose language is that of the love-in'. The two participant observation studies reported later support this observation.

Heroin

The full name of heroin is diacetylmorphine and it is a synthetic alkaloid produced by heating morphine and acetic acid. It was first synthesised in Germany in 1898. Morphine itself is a derivative of opium which comes from the *papaver somniferum*, a relative of the familiar garden poppy grown principally in the Middle East and in Southeast Asia. 'It was cultivated as early as 4000 B.C., undoubtedly for its pleasurable effects, in the Mesopotamian region of Sumer . . . from Sumer, knowledge of the narcotic qualities of the poppy spread through Asia Minor, Egypt and Greece' (Montagu 157:32). According to O'Donnell (164:2), heroin was originally thought to be non-addictive and a 'cure' for the opium habit. Its spread in America was assisted, until the passage of the Harrison Act in 1914 imposed controls, by the invention of the hypodermic syringe.

According to the World Health Organisation (213:13), drug dependence of the morphine type involves:

1 an overpowering desire or need to continue taking the drug and to obtain it by any means.

2 a tendency to increase the dose owing to the development of tolerance.

3 a psychic dependence on the effects of the drug related to a subjective and individual appreciation of its effects.

4 a physical dependence on the effects of the drugs.

However, this syndrome does not automatically occur as soon as a person starts taking heroin. Chein *et al.* (45:159) knew of individuals who had used heroin for several years on a more or less regular weekend basis and then ceased to use it, apparently without difficulty. Occasional users have also been reported in England by the Addiction Research Unit (132:1192).

According to Leech and Jordan (139:9), narcotics affect the central nervous system 'and depress the cerebral cortex and probably . . . the thalamus and hypothalamus. . . . Morphine and the opiates . . . slow down both mental and physical activity'; and (p. 44) 'after injection a great deal of the morphine content becomes concentrated in the liver and kidneys'. Other physical effects of heroin are, say Chein *et al.* (45: 356–8), pupillary constriction, constipation, amenorrhea and sexual apathy.

Heroin is taken in four ways: orally, by sniffing, by injection into the skin (skin-popping) and by injection into the bloodstream (main-lining). The latter is the method most frequently used by addicts, who, according to Leech and Jordan (139:43), dissolve the heroin and cocaine in water (usually from taps or lavatories) and inject it by a hypodermic syringe. In order to inject (139:44), 'a tourniquet is used . . . as the veins get used over and over again for injection they become scarred and unusable'. What happens after an injection is described by Chein (45:362):

> There is a transitory nausea which may particularly in the novice be followed by effortless and emotionally nondistressing vomiting. There is a period of maximal appreciation of the subtle effects of the drug. Some of these are body sensations, e.g. a feeling of impact in the stomach, bodily warmth, 'pins and needles' and itching sensations of a rather pleasant and eroticised nature, a feeling of lethargy, somnolence, relaxation and relief from tension or anxiety; and the experience of the 'high' . . . which is one of comfortable detachment from and lack of involvement in current experiences. The person feels 'out of this world', all his demands have been fulfilled, everything is taken care of. . . . Following the period of maximal appreciation of the effects of the drug there is a gradual return to the 'normal' state.

As a corollary to these Rathod (170:1412) lists the outward symptoms of a patient two to three hours after an injection, while he is 'high'. They are: 'small pupils, looks dreamy, and detached, fresh injection mark, doesn't want a proper meal, rubbing of eyes, chin and nasal area, slow and slurred speech, scratching of arms and legs and areas where clothes rub, resents being disturbed and spoken to, avoids noise and other strong stimuli, wakefulness interrupted by drowsiness'. Rathod (170:1412) goes on to list the following characteristics as being associated with the coming down from the high: 'wants to be left alone, gets very irritable, fidgeting with hands, paces up and down, cannot concentrate and perspires'. The 'high' described by Chein et al. (45:362) is not necessarily achieved by all addicts either because of an insufficient dosage or because the high might only be appreciated by very deviant individuals (Willis 208:221).

We have already seen that some heroin users remain for a considerable period of time as occasional users only. If the drug is taken frequently, tolerance soon occurs, and the patient has to increase the dosage to continue to get a 'high', till eventually, according to D. C. Cameron (34:315), the euphoriant effect is finally lost and the person continues to take drugs to feel 'normal' and avoid withdrawal symptoms. As Scher (177:542) says, the addict struggles with the three-pronged issue of maintaining euphoria, limiting tolerance and avoiding withdrawal.

The natural course of addiction, continues Scher (177:544), involves first a narrowing of interests and friends, then a period of isolation before a reorganisation of goals, way of life and relationships. Willis (208:225) supports this observation, reporting that some addicts spend literally all their time thinking about heroin, talking about it, getting it and taking it: all in the company of other addicts whose behaviour replicates and reinforces their own. The observable characteristics of this way of life are (Rathod 170: 1413): 'blood spotting on clothes, unexpected absences from home, sleeps out, the receiving and making of frequent telephone calls'. When addicts become addicted to this way of life they are twenty times as likely to die as their non-addicted peers (James 123:395). In America Louria (149:16–17) reports that in the period from 1954 to 1965 over 2000 deaths were caused by narcotic's overdose in New York city alone—'it is estimated that 1 per cent (of addicts) die every year from overdoses'. The dangers which lead to these deaths are: overdosing, which leads to respiratory inhibition, coma or death; disturbances in bodily functioning; risk of infection from the use of unsterilised water and needles and the sharing of syringes.

On the other hand not all heroin-takers end up devoting their lives to the pursuit of the drug. Besides the occasional users there are some addicted professional people who use the drug regularly with comparatively little social or mental deterioration. It has also been argued that addicts mature out of their addiction. In fact Chein *et al.* (45:356/359) comments that much of the deterioration seen in many of the addicts is due to the life they are forced to live rather than to the drug itself. He says that the danger of addiction to the opiates resides primarily in the person and not in the drug.

Summary

It can be seen, therefore, that the effects and patterns of drug usage depend not only on the drug itself but also on the person who takes the drug, the number of times he has taken it, the setting in which it is taken, and so on. It is because of the fact that social and psychological factors play an important part not only in drug usage but also in determining drug effects that studies that include these factors are needed. This is one of the reasons for this study. The other, and perhaps more important reasons, will be taken up in Chapter Two.

TERMINOLOGY

Tolerance. This term refers, according to Leech and Jordan (139:10), to the fact 'that more and more of the drug is needed in order to produce the same effect'. A similar definition is given by Isbell and White (119:558) who define tolerance as 'a decreasing effect upon repetition of the same dose of a drug'.

Withdrawal symptoms. These are the reactions of the body when deprived of a drug on which it is dependent. Withdrawal symtoms, according to Willis (207:113), include (for heroin) restlessness and irritability, stomach cramps, nausea, vomiting and diarrheoa.

Dependence. Before 1964 there were two terms in current use to explain the relationship between a person and his continued use of a drug. They were 'addiction', which referred to a state of periodic or chronic intoxication produced by the repeated consumption of a drug, and 'habituation', which was used to refer to people who took drugs frequently and consistently but showed no physical dependence upon them. In 1964 the World Health Organisation (213:9) decided to do away with these two terms and replace them with the common term 'dependence'. This was because it was realised that each type of drug produced a different pattern of dependence which could be either or both of a physical or a psychological nature. Leech and Jordan (139:14–16) define the terms as follows: 'Psychological dependence means that the user has produced a habit of using the drug while physical dependence means that the drug produces physical tolerance.' Physical dependence, according to Willis (208:221), is usually measured by the appearance of withdrawal distress when the drug is withheld.

THE LAW AND DRUGS

As regards the law and opiates, Gillespie *et al.* (89:156–7) say:

The so-called British system of control is old and has remained essentially unchanged since 1926. In that year a committee of medical men forming the Rolleston committee interpreted the Dangerous Drugs Law to mean that a drug addict is a sick person, and should be allowed drugs when 'the patient while capable of leading a useful and relatively normal life when a certain minimum dose is regularly administered becomes incapable of this when the drug is entirely discontinued'.

The specific Act which until recently has covered the opiates and cannabis is the Dangerous Drugs Act 1965 (61a), which limits possession to manufacturers, dispensers and medical practitioners, and gives the police powers to arrest anyone else on reasonable suspicion of unlawful possession. Maximum penalties are, on summary conviction, a £250 fine or one year's imprisonment. The Dangerous Drugs Act 1967 (61b) has restricted the prescribing of heroin to a number of doctors at special hospital clinics and prevented general practitioners from prescribing.

Amphetamines and LSD are covered by the Drugs (Prevention of Misuse) Act 1964 (66) which, while similar to the Dangerous Drugs Act 1965, has slightly different maximum penalties.

It is interesting to compare these penalties with those given in America. According to Louria (149:53) the 1956 Narcotic Control Act is the present basis for the laws relating to heroin use. Its provisions include penalties for the possession of narcotic drugs and marijuana: for the first offence 2–10 years, rising to 10–40 years for a third offence; while a person convicted of selling heroin to someone under 18 is subject to an imprisonment, for a first offence, ranging from ten years to life. The average sentence in 1964 was just under six years. Louria goes on to say that amphetamines, barbiturates and LSD are covered by the 1966 Drug Abuse Amendment which includes first offence penalities of £1000 maximum or one year's imprisonment for illicit manufacture, illegal sale or diverting drugs into the illicit market.

Probably the main effect of the harsher American legislation has been in the field of heroin addiction. In England, if the addict signs on at a hospital treatment centre he will receive a regular free supply of heroin and there is no need for him to indulge in criminal activities. In America the only way an addict can obtain heroin is on the black market. This normally results in the addict having to turn to crime to pay for his heroin supplies. Legislation obviously therefore forces addicts in England and America to adopt different life styles.

As regards the international situation Louria (149:52) says that 'international control is vested in three units operating under the auspices of the U.N. Existing treaties and international agreements, unfortunately, have been less than successful. Opium production continues at an excessive rate . . . the U.N. supervisory bodies have grossly inadequate enforcement powers.'

2 Reasons for the survey

THE SIZE OF THE PROBLEM

Drugs, particularly the narcotics, have been used throughout the world for thousands of years. Up to the eighteenth and nineteenth centuries their usage was concentrated in the Middle and Far East. Since then their widespread use has reached America and, more recently, England. Fort (81:130) estimated that in 1962 there were in the world perhaps 5 million abusers of sedatives, tranquillisers and stimulants and 10 million non-medical or illicit users of narcotics. Fort also estimated that those who repeatedly use the LSD type drugs probably number hundreds of thousands. Winick (211:20) estimates that 200 million persons throughout the world use marijuana.

Within the Western world the drugs problem reached America first in the late nineteenth century, when the discovery of heroin and that of the syringe followed closely upon one another. Despite a most punitive attitude since 1914 by the government towards drug abuse it was estimated by the Federal Narcotics Bureau that in 1965 there were 55,899 drug addicts alone (*Time Life* (191:5) and there were obviously an inestimable number of users in the other drug categories.

The problem in England is of a much more recent origin. Bewley (18:1) in 1965 wrote:

> Until recently . . . there was very little addiction among those who had obtained drugs from any illicit source. The situation has now changed. There has been a marked increase in opiate addiction among young people. There has also been a similar increase in the misuse of amphetamines by young people and the third noticeable change is that cannabis has been introduced into the country. Until a few years ago misuse of cannabis was almost non-existent. These three types of drugs have mostly been used by adolescents.

Further evidence as to the timing of the English problem is shown by the fact that the Brain Committee of 1961 (101:16) could conclude that in Great Britain the incidence of addiction to drugs controlled under the Dangerous Drugs Act 1951 was still very small, and traffic in illicit supplies was almost negligible, cannabis excepted. Yet by 1964 the Brain Committee had to be reconvened because of the rise in the number of non-therapeutic addicts.

It is very difficult to estimate how many people use each of the different drugs in Great Britain. To take each of the drugs in turn:

Heroin

Up to 16 April 1968, when the prescribing of heroin was limited to treatment centres, there was no official register of the number of heroin addicts in England. Before then the only known record was kept by the Home Office. According to Bewley (18:2) this was compiled from various sources. The most important were routine inspections of retail pharmacists' records. The police also reported cases as did some hospitals, doctors and social workers. 'The annual statistics . . . show only those addicts known to have been taking drugs during the previous year.' However, Bewley (18:2) says these statistics are inaccurate because they do not include: first, those addicts in the early stages of their addiction who obtain all their drugs from addict friends or from a black market source; secondly, addicts who are permanently supplied by the black market; and thirdly, those who have been temporarily removed.

Given their limitations the Home Office figures have shown a steady increase in the number of addicts in England since 1959, especially in the younger age groups:

ADDICTS KNOWN TO THE HOME OFFICE

Age (Years)	1959	1963	1966	1967
Under 20	—	17	329	395
20–34	50	184	558	906
35–49	92	128	162	142
50 plus	278	298	286	279
Unknown	34	8	14	7
Total number of addicts	454	635	1,349	1,729
No. of heroin addicts	68	237	899	1,299

The high increase in the number of young people becoming addicted is shown by the fact that while in 1960 the average age of heroin addicts was 28·7 years by 1964 it had already fallen to 23·5 years of age. Two reasons are often given for this increase in the number of addicts in the early sixties. The first of these was the arrival of about seventy Canadian addicts who were escaping from the harsher Canadian drug legislation (James 123:393). The second was that an excessive amount of heroin was being prescribed by a small number of doctors (Brain Committee 102:11) and it was suspected that each known addict was supplying one or two others. It was not until recently that any figures were available to indicate the number of heroin users who were receiving their drugs from the black market created by the over-prescribing.

A number of studies have now thrown some light on this problem. A study in Crawley New Town, using five screening methods, found ninety-two possible cases of heroin use and (1:551) 'until we made our findings known to them, the Home Office knew of only eight cases of heroin abuse in Crawley'. The Addiction Research Unit (132:1190), in a study of a provincial town, found thirty-seven subjects who had taken heroin, their average age being 20·7.

Only five of the subjects in the Addiction Research Unit's study (132:1191) were obtaining their supplies upon prescription. These studies therefore indicate that the number of unknown heroin users was probably as large as suspected. With the enactment of the 1967 Dangerous Drug Act, which limited the prescribing of heroin and which made the notification of addicts compulsory, it might have been hoped that a more precise figure of the number of heroin users would be found. However, this would only have happened if the overprescribing had stopped and the irregular and black market supplied heroin users had registered at clinics or given up heroin use. The indications are, though, that overprescribing is still continuing.

It is therefore impossible to obtain an accurate estimate of the size of the problem in England. The latest official figures are that by 10 May 1968 (Jeffery, Hospital Centre Conference, 111:657), 1400 addicts, of whom 870 were heroin users, had registered at the treatment centre and that by 28 July (107) the number of registered addicts had risen to 1796. However, a still unknown number of people will be using heroin on a regular or irregular basis and these, even though they are using heroin irregularly, might well be psychologically, if not physically, dependent on the drug.

Cannabis

There has been no reliable, reported survey to find the incidence of cannabis use. There have been, however, a number of attempts to estimate the size of the problem. Bewley (18:5), for example, says that 'if it is assumed that for every conviction there are possibly ten or twenty people who are not convicted it would give a figure for regular cannabis users in England of about 30 per 100,000 population'. If one now takes the conviction figures for 1967 when there were 2393 offences under the 1965 Act to do with cannabis (110) then this gives a figure of 70 per 100,000 population. If it were also assumed that for every person who uses cannabis with some degree of regularity there were five people who took it occasionally, then one would get a figure of 350 per 100,000 population, that is about 170,000 people who have tried the drug. Indirect evidence that the problem is as large as this comes from: Wilson and Linken (209), who report that cannabis is available in the majority of large British cities; from Linken (146) who estimates that from 3 to 10 per cent of students have had drug experiences, and from the Wootton report (109: para. 36) where witnesses guessed that the number of people who used cannabis was between 30,000 and 300,000.

Hallucinogens

There are no estimates of the number of people using these drugs in this country. The only relevant observation is that hallucinogens seem to be taken mostly by those who use cannabis frequently.

Amphetamines

Bewley (18:7) says that there are no accurate figures and no careful studies have been done on the numbers using amphetamines. The only official figures available are those for offences against the 1964 Act which applies to both amphetamines and hallucinogens. In 1966 there were 1216 offences against the Act and in 1967, 2486 (110). That these are a gross underestimation of the true extent of the problem is shown by the fact that Bewley (18:7) estimates that perhaps between 100 and 200 per 100,000 of the population of the United Kingdom have taken these drugs illicitly. The only relevant study is that by Scott and Willcox (180:12) who found that 17 per cent of boys and 20 per cent of girls at a remand home had recently taken amphetamines.

General drug estimates

There have been a number of small studies which have asked questions about drug usage without specifying any particular drug. Binnie and Murdock (23) in a survey of all students in higher education in a Midland city found that 9·44 per cent of the sample had used drugs and that of the takers, 84 per cent had confined their activities to pep pills and cannabis, only 5 per cent had ever used opiates and only 11 per cent had tried LSD. Schofield (178: 177) included a question about drug-taking and found that 3 per cent of the boys and 2 per cent of the girls had tried drugs. The *Sunday Times* in May 1967 commissioned a survey aimed at being representative of all the single girls in Great Britain aged 18–29 with controls of age, class and religion. They found that 2 per cent of those aged between 18 and 19 had sampled a drug but only 1 per cent of the 25–29-year-old age group had. In a recent survey of headmasters[1] in an educational borough nine out of fifteen said that they had a drug problem of some sort. That the problem reaches as far down the age scale as school children is shown by the Binnie and Murdock study (23) where it was found that the majority of users in each category had already taken drugs before they arrived at university.

There are three general comments on the size of the problem. The first comes from Mr Deedes (63:3), speaking in Parliament on 31 May 1968, who said that there was a serious drug problem which included people aged between 13 and 16. A second comment comes from Mr Howell who reported in Parliament (112: 1260) 'that all but four educational authorities have now replied . . . none of them had firm evidence of drug addiction among school children or students, but a number reported youthful experimentation with what are known as soft drugs'. The final comment comes from Davies (62:2) who writes:

In the city of Cambridge for example there is little doubt but that several hundred persons at any one time may be taking drugs illicitly. As far as the East Anglian region is concerned there must be a total of several thousand persons, many of them young, who are taking drugs either regularly or from time to time. Of these perhaps twenty-five to thirty are taking heroin.

---

[1] As this report is confidential it is not included in the Bibliography.

CDS

This summary of the drug problem has concentrated upon the young at risk. This is not to deny that there is a drug problem with older people but in their case, they have usually 'become habituated to, and finally dependent upon, certain drugs [usually amphetamines and barbiturates] prescribed in the first place to them for an illness' (Davies 62:2). The misuse of heroin, cannabis, the hallucinogens and, to a large extent, the amphetamines, is concentrated among young people. It is with these people, who start taking drugs for non-medical reasons, that this survey is concerned.

The figures indicate that there does seem to be a widespread abuse of drugs among young people, including children still at school. However, as can also be seen, there are no accurate figures as to the depth of the problem and therefore there is a need for any survey which can yield information about the numbers involved and about other related issues.

THE NEED FOR RESEARCH

Very little is known about the reasons why people take drugs, and who takes drugs. Similarly very little is known about the best way to educate people about the dangers of drugs. As the review of the literature will show, there has been comparatively little sociological and psychological research in this area, and what there is has nearly all been done in America. Moreover, the bulk of the research has concentrated on the heroin problem to the exclusion of the others. Yet there is an urgent need for research, not only because of rising incidence figures, but also because as Binnie and Murdock (23) say: The present public concern with drug-taking in young people and the legal position of marijuana was characterised by an air of unreality mainly due to a lack of information. The World Health Organisation is aware of this need for research and suggests that it should follow these lines:

(i) fact finding with respect to incidence as regards sex, age, occupation, groups at risk and the drugs abused.

(ii) definition of 'use' and 'abuse' in different cultures.

(iii) investigation of cause-effect relationships based on:
 (a) sociological background;
 (b) medical, psychological, economic and cultural factors.

(iv) prevention by education and legislation. (W.H.O. Report No. 343 (215:11).)

In future studies attention should be focused on the following factors and their interaction:

1 antecedence of varying present-day beliefs and attitudes towards drug usage and drug users.
2 variations in social settings and drug effects.
3 characteristics of deviant, drug using subcultures. (W.H.O. Report No. 343 (215:13).)

Fort (81:141) advocates that countries should have drug programmes 'placing their major emphasis upon prevention... which will concentrate on education designed to change attitudes ... the programme should begin in the schools ... seeking to bring about an awareness of the potential dangers and the encouragement of moderation and self-control'. And, in a similar vein to the World Health Organisation, suggests (81:143) that research is needed in the following areas: estimates of the number of users, causes of the use and/or abuse including socio-economic, cultural, historical and psychological factors, drug effects and programmes of education. Louria (149:76), commenting on the American situation, says that attempts to prevent drug abuse by appropriate educational techniques are at present astonishingly feeble. Louria goes on to say that 'every school situated in areas indigenous to drug abuse should have teachers knowledgeable to explain to students the nature of drugs and the dangers inherent in their use'.

Similarly some feel there is a need for education in English schools. To quote Davies (62:16), 'education is almost certainly the most important factor in prevention. It should not begin later than at the beginning of secondary school'. The recent survey of headmasters recommended that a statistical survey be carried out in the schools in the area 'which would provide factual evidence of the pattern of drug taking. This would be valuable in enabling Health Education for young people to start from a basis of knowledge.'

However, as the drug problem in England is not yet as large as that in America it might well be that such a full scale educational programme would not at the moment be appropriate here. To make a decision on this, information is needed, not only on incidence figures, but also on the attitudes and the knowledge of those who take drugs and those who do not.

It is as an attempt to provide figures to answer some of these problems that this survey is being carried out. It cannot hope to provide answers to more than a small number of them but it will also try to act as a pilot study for further projects already being planned in this field, so that they will be able to choose points of particular significance and look at them in depth.

The survey will concentrate on school children. This is done because, as Davies (62:16) says, it will be in schools that an educational programme will start if it is found to be needed. It is important, therefore, to find out at what level such a programme should be aimed, what the attitudes are that it has to change, what knowledge has to be corrected and so on. As the drug-taking problem appears to have reached the school population it will also be possible to find some idea of its incidence there and also to discover some of the reasons why young people take drugs.

THE DANGERS OF RESEARCH

There are reasons why perhaps a research project might do more harm than good. The first of these is to do with publicity. As Scher (177:539) says there seems 'to be a proportionate increase in most processes of behaviour deviation almost in accordance with the attention directed at their eradication'. A similar point was made in a *Times* (192:11) editorial recently which said:

> Drugs have become the subject of total press and television exposure ... the press has been entirely justified in reporting the growing epidemic of drug taking ... yet when this has been said, it is clear that there has been some deliberate sensationalism and that the total effect of the campaign is very dangerous. .... The total effect has been to dramatise drug taking and almost certainly to spread rather than inhibit the habit. It has been like a vastly expensive advertising campaign with the slogan 'Drugs are bad for you'. This is an appeal rather than a deterrent to the masochistic element in many people, and to the desire of boys and girls to take exciting risks.

The argument against this is first, that till one has the facts, one doesn't know whether drugs are a problem or not. Secondly, there seems to be a degree of inaccuracy in some press reporting, but till reliable figures are available it is not possible to know to what extent, if any, the press is exaggerating the problem.

Another possible set of dangers which might ensue from this type of research, and which were in fact sometimes voiced by local Education Authorities and headmasters, are summarised by Leech and Jordan (139:78/79) who write that those who argue against children knowing about drugs claim '(*a*) that talking about drugs may make you want to experiment with them out of curiosity . . . and (*b*) that if you do not know the problem exists there is no point in drawing it to your attention'.

The answer to these arguments from Leech and Jordan (139:79) is that 'others believe there is greater danger in ignorance. . . . Sooner or later you may well be confronted with people taking drugs illegally and you will be better protected . . . by knowing the truth.'

Some headmasters though, while agreeing with the general need for a survey such as this, still felt that it would arouse interest within the school without the benefit of being explicit about the dangers of drug-taking. Attempts were therefore made to overcome these fears. First, headmasters were requested to talk about the survey, when describing it to their staff, in terms of being a general study of teenage problems. Secondly, the children themselves were never told that this was a survey about drugs.[1] Thirdly, the questionnaires were so designed as to give an impression that drug-taking was only one of a number of social problems that the survey was interested in. In fact only 3 per cent of the children, when measured by their comments at the end of the questionnaires, found out the true purpose of the study. A final precaution was that both the samples were tested just before half-term as it was felt that if the children dispersed soon after the questionnaire administration more interesting events would have become the focus of attention by the time school reconvened.

These precautions were satisfactory for most of the headmasters but for those who still had doubts one could only point out that in the schools where the questionnaires had already been filled in there had not been, as far as was known, any sudden outbreak of drug-taking. With these safety factors and because of the need to find out which school children, and in what numbers, were taking drugs and also in order that information for planning an educational programme could be obtained, it was felt that the advantages of a survey would outweigh any bad effects which might have occurred.

---

[1] See Appendix E for the introduction read out to the children at the beginning of the questionnaire administration.

3 A review of the relevant literature

The review of the literature will obviously centre on the reported work on drugs and drug-taking. However, research in a number of other areas, such as small group behaviour, personality, socialisation, etc., is also relevant to a study of drug-taking among school children. As it is impossible to review the literature in all these fields, it was decided to concentrate on the field of deviance which appeared to have the most direct bearing on this study. This means that research into other forms of addiction, such as gambling, has also been excluded from this review. However, as the available evidence indicated that the drug-taking at school level was a problem of experimentation rather than of addiction, it seemed more appropriate to concentrate on research into deviance than research into addiction. Relevant pieces of research in addiction and other areas, for example Veness's study of school leavers (198), will be referred to throughout the book, when their findings or their methodology are particularly relevant, even though they are not included in this chapter.

DRUGS AND DRUG-TAKING

This review of the literature on drug-taking will concentrate on the methodological aspects of the research projects while the findings of these projects will be discussed in detail in chapter 5, which deals with the formulation of the hypotheses.

As a large part of the reported research in this area is concerned with various attempts to treat and cure heroin addiction, it has little direct relevance to this thesis. Much of the rest of the literature is concerned with other aspects of heroin dependence, such as the personality profiles of addicts (98), and even most of these studies may not be directly applicable to the English scene as they were carried out on American addict populations. The reason why one cannot generalise from the American findings is that there are many differences between the English and the American heroin situations.

The first of these differences is concerned with the backgrounds of the typical addicts in both of the cultures. According to Fort (81:134), the approximately 100,000 illicit narcotic users in the United States are 'mainly young, unemployed, uneducated, male adults of Negro, Mexican or Puerto Rican ancestry, living in large urban slums and coming from culturally deprived homes'. In England, however, according to Leech and Jordan, addicts do not necessarily come from run down conditions, nor do the majority come from minority ethnic groups. In fact 'of the 709 heroin addicts in the United Kingdom who were first known to be addicted between 1955 and 1965, 587 were British born and 72 were Canadians' (139:51). A second difference which Leech and Jordan (139:49) point out is that the heroin available on the black market in America is 'diluted and mixed with other substances' and is 'therefore considerably weaker than that used in Britain'. A third difference is that in America, as heroin use is illegal, addicts have to indulge in a criminal style of life to support their addiction. Louria (149:19), for example, estimates that in New York an addict's habit costs more than $15 a day and to support it 'addicts commit approximately twenty per cent of the crimes against property . . . and eighty per cent of the prostitutes arrested are drug addicts'. In England, provided the heroin is obtained from a treatment centre, its possession is not illegal and as it is issued free of charge the addict is not forced into a life of crime. A final difference that is pointed out by Wilkins (205:93) is that the images of the drug, of its use and of the addicts differ in the two cultures.

Therefore it can be seen that at least in the field of heroin addiction, there appears to be a marked dissimilarity between the two addict populations and their life styles. This means that such studies as that of the personality or the environment of American heroin addicts, must be treated as pilot studies, and their results as hypotheses, to see what extent they are applicable to this culture. This review will therefore concentrate on English studies and will only include American studies where they are of particular significance.

In the other fields there do appear to be some points in common. As Edwards (69:425) says about America, 'there has been growing alarm about the increased use of amphetamines, barbiturates and tranquillisers and the cult of using psychedelic drugs among college students'. However, except for one or two studies like Blum's (24) on LSD usage, which will be discussed later, there is comparatively little work done in the non-heroin fields.

There has been very little research done into drug-taking in England and much of what there has been has concentrated on the problems of addiction. There are various reasons for this. First, the problem in England is of such recent origin that there has not been enough time for a body of research to accumulate. Secondly, it is only recently that social psychologists and sociologists have taken an interest in the area and extended the range of focus to cover all aspects of drug-taking. The third reason arises from the difficulty of having to work with illegal substances and ill-defined deviant populations.

The available drug literature can be classified as follows: research into drug effects, research into the treatment of addiction, animal research, comments by authorities on the drug scene, surveys of small groups of drug-takers and lastly large-scale studies of drug-taking populations. Only the last three categories have direct application to this study.

Drug effects

A limited review of the relevant literature has already been summarised in Chapter 1 where a brief description of each of the drugs was given. The aim was to be as objective and balanced as possible without in any way suggesting that this was a comprehensive account of the relevant information, which would be a full thesis in itself.

Treatment of addiction

The various attempts to treat addiction, for instance the use of methadone, are outside the direct concern of a thesis on why school children take drugs.

Animal research

Most of the work in this area has been concerned with the effects of the administration of different drugs on various species of animal. An example of this is Steinberg's research (187) on the effects of amphetamine-barbiturate drugs on rats in familiar and unfamiliar surroundings. This type of research has only limited applicability in suggesting reasons why school children would take drugs. This is because these reasons appear to involve an intricate balancing of a number of factors including attitudes to drug use, friendship patterns, relationships to parents and to the society at large, variables on which animal studies have little to contribute.

Comments

Although there is a dearth of actual research into the field of drug-taking the literature is full of comments upon the problems it raises. These are given by psychiatrists, priests, probation officers, social workers, members of parliament, newspaper journalists and lay people. Obviously there are wide discrepancies in the value of these comments. Some, like the article by Beresford Davies (62), are worthy of serious consideration because they appear to be based upon a knowledge and understanding of the field. Others, for example, will insist on making generalisations from only a small biased sample. All that can be done with these comments is to separate them out and retain only those which come from people who have been working for some time in the field and who have made an attempt to give an objective account about a particular point. This has been done, and, where relevant, the selected comments will be used as contributing data in the selection and formulation of hypotheses.

Small-scale studies

HEROIN

There are seven studies of institutionalised addicts that can be treated together. Bewley (19:808) and Frankau (82:1377-8), in articles on the responses of addicts to treatment, include sections on the characteristics of these patients. Garmany (85) gathered some simple statistics on 105 addicts attending a treatment centre, while Gillespie et al. (89:155) interviewed twenty-six addicts obtained from six different sources. Chapple and Gray (43), while reporting on a year's work at their clinic, describe some of the addict patients and de Alarcon and Rathod (1) report on the heroin addicts found in their Crawley investigation. Finally Kaldegg (125) lists some information on addict patients who have passed through the Cane Hill Addiction Unit.

All these studies have limited application. This is, first, because they simply list characteristics, such as the social class of a small sample of institutionalised addicts. This has no general application because no one knows what percentage of heroin users attend institutions, whether there are any differences between addicts who attend institutions and those who do not, or what differences there are between addicts who attend different institutions. Till these factors are known it is impossible to generalise from one study and all that can be said about each study is that it describes the type of addict who attends this type of institution. The second reason for their limited application is that in none of the studies are there control groups and therefore one does not know which characteristics are important in differentiating addicts from non-addicts.

One study of heroin addicts which overcomes the first objection is the interview study by the Addiction Research Unit (132:1190). This study interviewed all the people known to be using heroin in a provincial town who were resident there at the time. While this study has the advantage of at least providing a comprehensive picture of all the known addicts in one town it is also restricted in the application that can be made of the results. This is first, because the addicts in any one town are not necessarily like those in another. For example, if one takes the finding that heroin use spreads through friendship groups this might well have been a function of the fact that someone had to travel outside the town to bring in illegal supplies from London. However, in London itself, where heroin is probably more easily available, there would be a greater likelihood of being introduced to the drug by a casual acquaintance. This point is in fact made in a follow up article (217) which says:

It appears that much of their interaction was centred on the need to organise and obtain supplies which is no longer necessary since many of those concerned are on prescription. The overall pattern of frequent contact has now been replaced by more isolated meetings of small groups. It would appear that much of the meeting and interaction seems to have been based on drug need, rather than the satisfaction of inter-personal needs.

Secondly, the study had no control group. Therefore, though it is useful to know the social class of the addicts in the town, it would be much more useful if one also knew the social class of drug-takers who have not escalated, and of people who have been offered drugs and refused them. Thirdly, any study such as this which employs a large number of people as interviewers always runs the risk of unreliability arising from different interviewing styles. This to some extent was controlled in this study by the use of an interviewing schedule for the interviewers to follow. Another likely unreliability factor arises from the possibility that addicts will give different responses at different periods after fixing.

A final problem is that of validity. Do you know whether what the addicts say is the truth or not? For those addicts who were registered with a doctor or who are now registered at a clinic there is in fact an external source against which the information can be checked. However, if there are any discrepancies in biographical information it is not always possible to know which, if any, of the versions is true. In the Addiction Research Unit study these checks were applied where possible.

Therefore the research into heroin addiction in this country has concentrated so far on small-scale studies of highly selected groups of addicts, primarily on those who are institutionalised. While this has provided much useful background information about the addict population its utility for this study is limited to suggesting hypotheses, such as paternal deprivation, which should be tested. This restricted usage of the data is necessary because as there were no control groups it is impossible to know which of the characteristics of the addict population differentiate them from the non-addict population. Even if there are control groups it is usually difficult to know to what extent any differences were caused by the addiction process, and which pre-existed the addictive stage and might therefore have been causal factors contributing to it.

OTHER SMALL GROUP STUDIES

There have been a number of unrelated studies carried out on small groups of individuals. One such was a study carried out by the L.S.E. Social Psychology Department (16) in which forty-three drug-taking subjects were found through personal contacts and interviewed. The project was designed as a pilot to delineate clearer areas for further research and too much criticism should not be levelled at it. The authors themselves admit that the sample was probably overrepresentative of the middle classes. As it had no control group the primary analysis was to compare takers of different types of drugs and different frequencies of drug usage. However, to the extent that it is true that there are differences between the people who use one type of drug and those who use another and, if this sample tends to be drawn from just one group of the population (i.e. amongst people known to the interviewers), analysis results in the comparison of a typical user of one kind of drug with an atypical user of another kind. This argument would similarly apply to differences between frequencies of usage.

Another line of study is that carried out by probation officers or social workers on cases they come across in their work. There are a number of such unpublished studies but again they have limited application, first, because there is no control group so one does not know what, if anything, makes these subjects different from non-drug-taking peers, secondly, one cannot know if drug-takers who come before the courts are the same as those who are not caught; thirdly, drug-takers in one area are not necessarily typical of those in another.

Scott and Willcox (180:10–13), using urine tests as a means of discriminating amphetamine users, compared arrivals at a remand home who gave positive results with a set of controls. The authors found comparatively little difference between the two groups. This might be due to a number of reasons. First, as a urine test will only reveal whether amphetamines have been taken during the previous thirty-six hours it might well have been the case that the control group itself contained a high percentage of drug users. Secondly, as the control group were also delinquents, it might simply mean that deliquent drug-takers are no different from other delinquents. One cannot infer from this either that all drug-takers are delinquent or that no differences would be found between a group of non-delinquent drug-takers and their controls. In a similar study (10), forty-six drug-takers and fifty-four controls from a population of Borstal youths were compared on the personality test, the M.P.I., on the Smally test, on the I.P.A.T. Anxiety Scale questionnaire, on the Raven's Matrices Test, and on an abstraction test of verbal intelligence. No personality differences were found between the drug-takers and the controls, though the drug-takers scored significantly higher on the Raven's Matrices Test. However, these results suffer in interpretation from the same limitations as applied in the previous study.

A different type of study was a survey of headmasters by a city council health department, where a social worker tried to estimate the size of the problem in the area by talking to headmasters, visiting youth clubs, hospital clinics, etc. This approach will only give a very limited idea of the true extent of a problem, first, because various authorities are likely to differ in their interest in a problem and therefore in the extent of their knowledge about it; secondly, much of what they know is likely to be hearsay; and thirdly, there is usually no possibility of checking the accuracy or the validity of the information received from these sources.

A study done by Palmae (166:1074) on juvenile courts between April 1964 and March 1965 indirectly produced figures as to the incidence of drug cases. However, these figures have little meaning, first, because only a small percentage of those who commit delinquent acts are apprehended; secondly, because people often appear in courts outside the districts in which they live; and thirdly, because differences in court figures often appear to reflect a change in police interest in the topic rather than an actual change of drug usage.

In another study of Linken (146), 250 subjects under the age of 30 who attended a venereal disease clinic were asked if they had ever taken drugs. The 18·2 per cent who said yes were given questionnaires to fill in. Once again, all that this type of study can do is to describe characteristics of another biased sample of drug-takers. Schur (179) carried out a two-part study in England in 1958. The first part involved detailed interviews with a number of heroin addicts and the second a survey of drug-taking among young males in a London borough. Because of the changes in the drug-taking pattern in England in the early 1960s these studies are now of mainly academic interest. This is particularly true of the interviews with the addicts. In the second part Schur (179:235–40) interviewed 147 randomly selected residents of the borough of Willesden aged between 20·5 and 21 years of age. Only nine of the subjects reported any personal contact with cannabis or heroin. Schur adapted many of the scales used by Chein et al. (45), whose work will be discussed below, but they had often only a very small range of items. For example, there were only two questions to measure the subject's drug knowledge.

The last work in this section is an American study by Blum (24) which is interesting for its methodological aspects rather than for its findings. The aim of the study (24:20–37) was to find out about the use of LSD and its effects. The subjects were obtained, as in the previously discussed L.S.E. study (16), through personal contacts. Altogether there were ninety-two subjects who had taken LSD. These subjects came from five different groups of users: professional users, therapeutic users, experimental subjects, a religious-medical centre and informal black market users. Within these groups not all the subjects approached agreed to be interviewed. Ninety-two is, however, a very small proportion of all LSD users. Even though some attempt was made to stratify the sample, the members of each of the groups interviewed were not necessarily representative. Therefore the first criticism is that as one does not know to what extent this sample is representative of LSD users as a whole it is impossible to generalise from the results. Because of this limitation the main analyses, as in the L.S.E. study (16), are between subjects who took the drug regularly and those who had given it up, and between a group of regular LSD users and a control group selected on the basis of people known to the regular user who had been offered the drug and refused to take it. The danger of using this particular control group is that one might in fact be comparing two extreme groups: people who are in a position to be offered a drug and then refuse it might be a more extreme group than people who have never been offered a drug in the first place.

In this section, there are a number of studies which, while revealing facts about particular drug-taking groups, have little general applicability. Again, for the purpose of this study they are most useful for providing data for the design of hypotheses.

Large-scale studies

There is in fact a paucity of large-scale research in this field. The most comprehensive and best planned is that of Chein *et al.* (45) on New York heroin addicts, and Goldberg's studies (93, 94) of the Swedish drug problem.[1] There have been large-scale studies in other fields which have included a question on drug-taking, such as Schofield's study (178), and further large-scale surveys are being carried out in America but have not yet been completed.

Chein's work consists of an intensive study of drug-taking, with particular reference to heroin, in three boroughs of New York between 1949 and 1958. The study was done in three main parts. The first was concerned with finding out what made one area a high drug use area and another a low drug use area and included taking samples of school children in both areas.

The second part studied the importance of the individual's environment as a causative factor. In this part Chein compared fifty-nine institutionalised drug addicts who were not delinquent before they started drug use with forty-one institutionalised drug addicts who were delinquent prior to the onset of drug use and compared both of these with fifty institutionalised delinquents who were not heroin users. Finally he had a fourth group which acted as a control group and consisted of fifty-two non-delinquent, non-heroin users from the same type of neighbourhood. The third part of the study involved an analysis of drug-taking among street gangs in the three boroughs.

---

[1] Binnie and Murdock's study (23) of the attitudes to drugs and drug-takers of students at the university and colleges of higher education in an English Midland city should also be included in this section, but it was published too late to be considered in detail here.

The results of this survey will be included where relevant in the formulation of hypotheses. Whereas these results merit more consideration than others in the field for the thoroughness of the approach, the time gap from when the study was first done, means that by now the results probably for America but most definitely for England have to be treated as hypotheses in need of retesting.

The main criticism of this type of study of Chein's is one basic to all cross-sectional designs, namely that on many of the variables, for example attitudes to drugs, if one finds a difference between the drug-takers and their controls one does not know whether the difference is due to the drug-takers having taken drugs or whether it existed beforehand and was therefore one of the reasons why these people took drugs.

The aims of the Swedish study (93 and 94:1) are:

1 To give quantitative data on incidence and prevalence of use and abuse of narcotic drugs with respect to:
   (a) the development of the situation in Sweden;
   (b) the actual state in various strata of the population, e.g. in hospitals, among groups with a criminal background and in different social sub-groups with varying characteristics;
   (c) the possible differences in types and patterns of drug abuse among various groups, with regard to age, involvement of juveniles, criminal background, and other social and sociological background data.

2 To characterise the present situation and its consequences from medical, legal and social points of view.

3 To elucidate some factors involved in the dynamics of the present situation.

Among the many studies carried out within this programme, five were on adolescents, two of them concentrating upon school children. In the first, 130,061 pupils, aged 14–19 and comprising 11 per cent of the total population in the classes concerned, were interviewed. As schools were invited to write in for questionnaires, the sample was not representative. The second study took all 16-year-old pupils in Stockholm, i.e. 8353 subjects. This study compared pupils from the school with the highest drug use with those in the school with the lowest incidence of drug use.

Because the programme is not yet completed, and because the studies have not been presented in all their detail, it is not possible to be critical of them. However, any programme of such magnitude which will permit multifactorial analyses to be carried out is likely to produce a wealth of findings with direct relevance to Swedish conditions and, because of cultural differences, of indirect relevance to other cultures.

Conclusion

This review of the literature has shown that few studies have direct bearing on the problems of discovering drug-taking patterns among school children. Much of the reported work is American and because of various differences in the two cultures the results of these studies can be considered only as hypotheses to be tested in the English culture. It is because the American results are to be utilised only as aids in the formation of hypotheses that their analysis has been comparatively brief. The research that has so far been done in England has concentrated primarily on small groups of drug-takers and because of the relative paucity of its size and execution it can do little more than indicate the characteristics of different drug-taking populations and suggest further hypotheses worth testing.

PROBLEMS OF DRUG RESEARCH

As has been shown it is quite easy to criticise the research that has so far been done. It is more difficult to be constructive. This is because there are serious methodological difficulties in working in the drug field. First, there is the problem of sampling an unknown population. If one is solely interested in heroin addiction it is possible to take a sample of addicts who are registered at a clinic but this only samples institutionalised addicts and ignores those who obtain their supplies illegally and those who are only occasional users. With the other drugs there is not even an institutionalised population on which to start. One does not know who the drug-takers are. One possible solution would be to take a representative sample of young people. But the difficulty is that many of the people who take drugs do not appear on the normal lists from which representative samples are drawn. Many drug-takers have no set jobs, no permanent addresses, are not on electoral rolls, do not appear on the streets at normal times and so on. Another alternative is to take a small area, as Schur (179) and the Addiction Research Unit's (132) studies did, but unless one does many of these small intensive studies one does not know how representative one area is of others.

Secondly, even if a representative sample is drawn up, because of the nature of the topic, many of the selected people and/or authorities are unlikely to cooperate. This happened in the second sample drawn up in this study.

Thirdly, there is the difficulty of control groups. As has been seen, if there is no control group this will reduce the value of the data obtained. The problems of drawing controls from institutions for institutionalised addicts and from people who have refused drugs for non-institutionalised drug-takers, have already been considered. Another suggestion for a control group is to get the siblings of drug-takers because this serves to treat family and background factors as controlled variables. However, not only do many drug-takers not want their families involved but it is questionable whether the family environment is in fact standard for all siblings within a family. A different method of obtaining a control group was that used in a study of American addicts by Gerald and Kornetsky (87). In this study controls were obtained from non-drug-using acquaintances and friends of the heroin addict. The controls were then matched with the addicts on a number of variables.

A final difficulty is that the ideal study, to reveal significant differences between drug-takers and non-drug-takers, is a longitudinal design, where subjects are first tested before they start taking drugs, while in the middle school years, and then followed up over a number of years. Only in this way can one determine which factors existed before addiction started. However, though such studies have been planned they have not so far been carried out because of the newness of the problem, lack of resources and staff, difficulties of confidentiality and because there is still much useful data which can be obtained by simpler means.

The design most frequently used in surveys of this kind, and the one used in this case, is a cross-sectional design which compares groups of subjects on different points at the same period of time. The difficulties in interpreting the results of this type of work have already been discussed. This difficulty does not apply to the same extent in this survey because, when dealing with subjects who have just started to try drugs, the actual drug-taking behaviour will have had comparatively little effect on most of the variables to be measured.

In conclusion, therefore, it must be stressed that the drug field is not an easy one for research and to criticise everything as being useless is to overlook the fact that any information is better than no information at all.

Dds

DEVIANCE

Two recent works, by A. K. Cohen (49) and by West (203), have comprehensively summarised both the theoretical approaches and the reported researches in this field. The conclusions one can draw from these two books are of particular relevance here.

West (203:99), in his review of the theories of deviance, comments that

> an outstanding weakness of the social theories of delinquency is the absence of factual evidence in support of any one in preference to the rest. The few hard facts that have been established, such as the social class neighbourhood distribution of offences, are for the most part consistent with all the theories.

He concludes that

> in short, in explaining persistent delinquency, as with all unusual behaviour patterns, one has to take into account a great variety of factors: social, individual, biological and environmental. The simple answer is a myth (203:295–6).

This type of conclusion is supported by the variety of theories that Cohen (49) covers (control, defence mechanism, anomie, reference group, cultural transmission and interactionist) where each in some way contributes to the understanding of the problem but none in itself is sufficient to explain all cases. This multiple causal pattern reinforces the intention that the survey should examine as many variables as possible: as from a theoretical point of view, no particular factor seemed to be more important than others.

An entirely different conceptual approach to the analysis of drug-taking, and one worth mentioning, is the perceptual theory of Wilkins (205:91). This states

(*a*) that certain types of information in relation to certain systems lead to more acts being defined as deviant;
(*b*) the individuals involved in the acts so defined are 'cut off from the values of the parent system by the very process of definition;
(*c*) ... they begin to see themselves as deviant ...';
(*d*) the deviant groups will develop their own values.

This leads to more actions being taken against deviants who become further alienated and more deviant, which leads to more actions being taken against them and so on. While this type of theory can explain in part an increase in the size of a deviant population it is not so relevant to the problem of why people take drugs in the first place.

As regards the practical studies in the field, those which have already been reviewed by West (203) will be included, where relevant, in Chapter 5. In particular, two studies of teenage behaviour have played an important part in the design of the present study even though they are not directly studies of deviance. The two studies are Schofield's *The Sexual Behaviour of Young People* (178) and the Government Social Survey's study (95) of cigarette smoking among school children. Both are primarily studies aimed at finding the normal behavioural pattern of teenagers. However, the subjects who turned out to be most sexually experienced and who were the heaviest smokers were definitely deviant in terms of the norms of behaviour of their peer group. It appeared, therefore, that any differences found between these two groups of deviant subjects and their peers would be worth following up in a study of school children and their behaviour in the deviant behavioural field of drug-taking.

Schofield (178:283) drew his sample from three sources, one of these being from school attendance lists. In fact 40 per cent of boys and 18 per cent of the girls in his sample were still at school (178:153). Schofield compared subjects of differing degree of sexual experience on leisure activities, relationships with parents, amount of time spent at home, type of school attended, whom they referred to with a personal problem, the amount they drank, delinquency and attitudes to life. The main relevance of Schofield's work to this study is that in nearly all these factors he found significant differences between sexually experienced and sexually inexperienced subjects. The survey into cigarette smoking among male school children carried out by the Government Social Survey (McKennell and Bynner 153:29) had a sample of 5601 subjects. The subjects were all in their first four years at secondary school and were selected from six types of secondary school: mixed grammar, boys only grammar, mixed comprehensive, boys only comprehensive, mixed secondary modern, and boys only secondary modern. This study, using questionnaires rather than interviews, covered much of the same ground as Schofield's work. In addition the study used semantic differential scales to measure a person's self perception in relation to their perception of drug-takers and had other scales measuring attitudes to smoking. The report shows that the survey found significant differences between smokers, triers and non-smokers on all these variables. Both these studies also made important methodological contributions to the present survey, particularly in reference to the design of the questionnaires. This will be enlarged upon in the next chapter.

Conclusion

On a theoretical level there are many explanations of deviance but so far there is insufficient evidence to choose between these explanations except to say that deviance appears to be multi-determined. On a practical level two recent large-scale surveys have found significant differences on a number of variables between deviant young people and their peers.

4 Basic field work

The final hypotheses tested in this survey were arrived at after:

1 a review of the literature on drugs and drug-taking.
2 a review of the literature on deviance.
3 talking to people working in the drug field.
4 talking to a wide range of drug-takers.
5 two participant observation studies.
6 a pilot study.

The first two points were discussed in the previous chapter and the pilot study will be discussed in Chapter 6. This chapter will consider the remaining three points and show how they were important in providing information from which hypotheses, as to why people take drugs, could be drawn up.

WORKERS IN THE FIELD

Interviews were held with a number of people who worked with drug-takers. The people interviewed included: three psychiatrists who had hospital clinics for addicts, another psychiatrist in general practice who treated addicts,[1] a prison psychiatrist, a prison psychologist, a number of detached social workers and a sociologist who was doing research into heroin addiction.

These discussions were particularly helpful in providing background information about the general drug problem in England and about the heroin problem in particular. They also helped to clarify the areas where more research was needed.

---

[1] This was before the 1967 Dangerous Drugs Act.

DRUG-TAKERS

Through the services of friends and acquaintances, informal and completely open-ended interviews were had with about 150 people who had taken between them nearly all the conceivable combinations of different drugs. The inteviewees included university students, artists, known heroin addicts and prison inmates. These interviews proved particularly useful in finding out about patterns of drug abuse, drug-taking habits, attitudes of drug users to drugs and to life in general and about drug-taking slang.

PARTICIPANT OBSERVATION STUDIES

For a number of reasons it appeared important to supplement a review of the literature with actual observations of drug-taking behaviour. The first reason was that as most of the literature deals solely with the problems of heroin addiction, there is comparatively little recorded about the behaviour of people who take drugs other than heroin on a regular or occasional basis. The second reason for the studies was that as the conditions under which a drug is taken can influence its effects, it seemed essential to supplement the laboratory studies with actual observations of drug-taking. A third reason was to discover whether the explanations for taking drugs that subjects gave during interviews were in fact the same as they used amongst themselves. A fourth reason was to obtain possible hypotheses concerning differences between non-drug-takers and drug-takers. A fifth reason was to gain information about the attitudes drug-takers held towards drugs and towards life in general. A final reason was to become familiar with the drug-taking culture and its language.

The observed groups

As it appeared unlikely that any school children would be heroin addicts an attempt was made to gain admittance to groups which used the amphetamine, cannabis and hallucinogenic types of drugs. Eventually it became possible to observe one group where cannabis and LSD were the drugs most frequently used and a second group where pep pills were the most common.

The first group (Cannabis) LSD

The main members of the group, being in their mid- to late twenties, were slightly older than would have been liked. Another disadvantage of this group was that three of its four main members were foreigners. However, through this nucleus it was possible to come into contact with a wider range of drug users. The group centred around one flat where the four main members lived. There were two males, a camera man and a designer, and their girl friends. Other members of the group were met at the flat or at parties to which the observer went with the group.

The second group (pep pills)

This group was centred round a discotheque which was run with the express purpose of assisting young people in distress. It therefore attracted a very biased sample of youngsters, ranging in age from 15 to 30 with the mean about 20. As regards age, therefore, it was closer than the first group in providing subjects nearer to the school children in which the survey was interested. The observer came to know the people who ran the club and was invited to come down and see what happened. This resulted in the observer attending the club on a number of Saturday nights, when he helped in the running of the club by working the cash register, washing up, etc.

Problems of participant observation studies

There are a number of methodological problems attendant on participant observation studies. One of these is that the observer, through his interaction with the group, will change its pattern of behaviour. This was in fact only a difficulty with the first group, because in the second group the observer was never in any way a member of the club, and, being largely ignored, had no discernible effect upon what happened there. To minimise the problem in the first group the observer called at the flat on random occasions without prior warning. By doing this it was hoped that this would reduce the likelihood of the group restructuring its behaviour to take account of the presence of the observer.

Another difficulty is that the extent to which the observer is accepted as a member of the group will determine what he will be told and allowed to see. As Becker (12:72) points out, one of the necessary functions of an illegal drug using group is to prevent non-users from knowing one is a user. Therefore to be able to see what happens the observer must not be perceived as being a threat to the group. In the first group the observer seemed to be accepted to fairly full confidentiality almost immediately, for example he was invited to spend the night there on his first visit. This was probably because his initial contact was with the unofficial leader of the group. In the second group the observer always remained outside the group and to this extent he only saw what went on within the club premises, where, probably because of his association with the club leaders, he did not appear to be perceived as a threat.

A third problem concerns the reliability of data. There are three parts to this problem. First, if there is only one observer there must, owing to the factor of selective perception, always be a problem of reliability. Secondly, the longer the gap between the observation and the recording of the event the greater the unreliability owing to selective recall. Thirdly, as only samples of the behaviour of the two groups were observed there must be doubts as to how representative these observations were of the group's total behaviour. In both studies, the first unreliability factor must be accepted as a necessity of the situation. The second factor, the problem of selective recall, was different for the two groups. In the first group, because the observer was accepted in the role of a friend and not in that of an observer, it was impossible to record events as they occurred. The alternative adopted was to write down as fully as possible everything that had occurred on each visit at the first available opportunity after leaving the group. By this method it was possible to obtain a reliable recording of the actual drug use that occurred, but it was not possible to report, with complete accuracy, all of the conversations about drugs that had ensued. In the second group, where there was less drug-taking and less talk about it, the principal aim of the observer was to try to gain general impressions about a way of life that these youngsters lived and the reasons why some of them took drugs. Therefore, as no attempt was made to record everything that occurred and as any impressions were noted immediately, the second unreliability factor is not relevant here.

In the first group, an attempt was made to overcome the third part of the problem of reliability, that of representativeness, by paying random visits to the group. In the case of the second group the study is only representative of the behaviour of the members while they were in the club. As regards the members' behaviour outside the club this could only be inferred from conversations with, and overheard remarks of, members and to this extent must be suspect on grounds of both reliability and validity.

The study of the first group

The group was visited on six occasions. The study had then to be curtailed because to remain an accepted visitor the observer would have been compelled to adopt the group's norms and life style.

VISIT ONE

People seen. Observer arrived at about 9.15 p.m. The four main members were there as well as two Americans. Shortly after the two Americans left, a painter dropped in and the two girls went out for a while to a night club.

Drug-taking pattern. On arrival the two girls were smoking cannabis. The camera man had been smoking it earlier in the day. When the Americans left they were given some cannabis. The painter was offered some LSD but he refused to take it. The two girls on return said they had been smoking hashish at a night club where they had met a friend who had taken two pills of LSD and was 'out of her mind'.

VISIT TWO

People seen. Observer arrived in the evening. The two male group members were there with another girl. Later the designer took this girl home. Later the designer's girl friend arrived back at the flat.

Drug-taking pattern. The camera man had been smoking cannabis throughout the day and was still under its effects.

VISIT THREE

People seen. The camera man, the designer's girl friend and the observer attended an auction in the country. In the evening they attended the theatre with the designer and two other friends. After the theatre the group, minus the two friends, moved on to a party. There were about thirty people present of whom about twenty seemed to be acquaintances of the group. After a short time the designer's girl friend returned home and the designer and the camera man went and brought back to the party two girls whom they had met on a recent trip to Paris.

Drug-taking pattern. Before setting off for the auction in the country the two group members both took part of an LSD pill and were experiencing its effects during the whole day. At the party in the evening three people were smoking cannabis and two were using a white powder. The two girls who joined the party later had had their first experience of LSD that day.

VISIT FOUR

People seen. Observer arrived in the evening. The camera man's girl friend and the designer were present. A female actress called in and left with the designer. Shortly afterwards two friends of the camera man's girl friend called in. The camera man came in and left almost immediately for a dinner engagement. Later in the evening the designer and the actress returned for a few minutes.

Drug-taking pattern. No one took any drugs during this visit.

VISIT FIVE

People seen. On arrival only the camera man was present. After a while his girl friend and a male friend of theirs came in and shortly afterwards the designer and a friend of his came in.

Drug-taking pattern. Both the designer and his friend were in the middle of an LSD trip. It was the friend's first experience with the drug. The rest then decided they wanted to take drugs but on reaching their supply they found someone had stolen it.

VISIT SIX

People seen. On arrival in the evening at the flat, the camera man, the designer and a girl were present.

Drug-taking pattern. No drugs were taken on this visit.

ALL VISITS

Drug-taking pattern. On all the visits, even when no drugs were taken, there was considerable conversation about drugs. These involved their usages, effects and the drug-taking habits of acquaintances. During these conversations the designer said that he had taken LSD twelve times and his girl friend said that she had taken it eleven times.

Findings

REASONS FOR TAKING DRUGS

(*a*) The smoking of cannabis was so common and so much an accepted part of life that no justification was ever given for its use. All the argument for and against drug use centred on LSD.

(b) LSD makes the world look different. Because group members found this interesting they nearly always went out into the everyday world while under its influence.

(c) LSD is useful to solve personal conflicts. It was believed that while under its influence one was able to see one's conflicts more clearly and objectively.

(d) LSD makes one more creative and productive. The camera man, for example, felt that he had compressed many months' work into one and that his mind was working on such a level that he could come to grips with any subject in a short period of time and pierce to the centre of any argument very quickly.

(e) Because LSD was so much part of the 'scene' that it was impossible to understand the scene unless one tried the drug.

(f) Because LSD would help to overcome blocks in an artist's work.

(g) As an aphrodisiac. Cannabis was also used in this way.

REASONS FOR NOT TAKING LSD

(a) Because of its reactions.
(b) Because of the risk of bad trips.

EFFECTS OF THE DRUG

It is difficult under any conditions to record drug effects in a meaningful manner. This is particularly true of the participant observation situation when it is not possible to ask too many direct questions. One of the main difficulties is that the drug experience is a comparatively solitary one which has limited meaning to someone who has not been in a similar state. Also it appears that much of what occurs, in terms of altered sensations, is not readily communicable on a verbal level. For example, it is comparatively meaningless to be told that the effects of cannabis are 'being high', 'better communication with one's fellows', 'that life was great when I was turned on', etc. One report which supported the account of depersonalisation that occurred under LSD came from the designer's girl friend who, while under the influence of the drug, commented that she was feeling with all parts of her body and didn't know what part she was.

From a strictly external, behavioural point of view the only noticeable effect came when one of the subjects was observed on his first LSD trip. On a previous meeting this person had been very cocky, dominating and egocentric but on this occasion he was smiling, happy, boyish and shy.

ATTITUDES TO THE POLICE

During the first visit there was a general conversation about police. The Americans said that when the cops picked you up stateside you never knew whether they were going to ask you to bend over, let you go, ask for a bribe or what. The camera man said that the police were not like that over here but he did complain that the heat was on. For example, he said that he suspected that the flat was watched and the phone tapped. This threat was obviously treated as a reality because the group had codes for talking about drugs over the phone. The conversation also discussed the dogs the police used to detect cannabis and of possible ways to frustrate them.

GENERAL LIFE STYLE

(a) All subjects tended to live very impulsively. That is, they would do whatever the immediate situation offered rather than carry out longer term plans. For example, on three occasions plans were made for dinner that evening yet when during the day something else cropped up which appeared more interesting, the original plan was always dropped, irrespective of any inconvenience it might have caused.

(b) The arts was held to be something particularly meaningful, whether they were photography, cinema, theatre, pop music, etc. These activities were held in some way to be the accepted pursuits for people moving in these circles.

(c) Life was lived at a furious pace. People were always on the move to some place or to see someone. It was as if the pace itself gave some sort of meaning to life.

(d) There was an emphasis upon the exploration of one's own personality as being more important than worldly possessions.

The study of the second group

Twelve visits were paid to the club. The pattern of events was similar on each occasion. The observer would arrive at about 11 p.m. and leave around 4 a.m. the following morning. During the time he was there the observer would help out in the club, observe what was happening and talk either to members or to the social workers who ran the club.

THE CLUB

The club had a membership numbering in thousands. On a Saturday night there would be anything from 150 to 400 people present. The club was on two floors. On the lower there was a juke-box, a space for dancing, a coffee-bar and a small number of tables and chairs. Upstairs there was a small restaurant which was run by members of the club.

DRUG-TAKING

There was, in theory, a ban on drugs in the club. On the one police raid the club experienced no drugs were found. This did not mean that no club members took drugs. First, in defiance of the ruling, a few members took pep pills or fixed heroin on the club premises. Secondly, drugs were easily obtainable in other clubs in the neighbourhood. A number of members, during the course of the evening, would go to these clubs, buy drugs, take them out-side, and then return while 'high' to the first club. Quite surprisingly though, the percentage of members who took drugs on a regular basis appeared to be quite small. This was surprising because not only were drugs freely available in the general area but some people who frequented the club were known to be drug pushers.

The type of drug most frequently used appeared to be pep pills. Some members said they took LSD. Only a few seemed to smoke cannabis. Whereas they all seemed to know of heroin addicts, some of whom occasionally came into the club, heroin seemed to be feared by most members who regarded addicts as foolish people.

GENERAL LIFE STYLE

(a) The simple fact that many members stayed at the club all Saturday night says something about their home relationships. From general conversation it in fact seemed that a large number of the younger members did come from disturbed family backgrounds and it was often to escape from these that they stayed out all night.

(b) The members were very clothes conscious. They were also very interested in popular music, the juke-box had the latest hits and members frequently attended pop concerts.

(c) The members seemed to come generally from a more working-class environment than did members of the first group. Also in comparison to the first group where members spent a lot of time discussing theories about life, members of the second group appeared to be primarily concerned with people and things.

General discussion about the two groups

It is interesting to conjecture why the two groups had a different drug-taking pattern. One reason to explain this was that differences in the life styles of the two groups necessitated the use of different drugs. In the second group there was an emphasis upon physical activity. The group had to stay awake all night because, after 11 p.m. when public transport stopped, there was no way for them to get home, even if they wanted to. Staying awake involved dancing, talking and being generally on the move. In this case the drug needed would be one which gave a temporary burst of physical energy, i.e. a pep pill. On the other hand the first group concentrated upon problems of self-discovery and creative insights. The drugs which assist these types of discovery are cannabis and the hallucinogens.

These two studies showed that it was impossible to talk in terms of a common drug-taking culture as these two groups had comparatively little in common. Any attempt to have classified them together would have resulted in a gross oversimplification of the problem.

Value of the studies

It is possible to look at this in terms of the reasons for the studies:

1 To obtain information concerning non-heroin drug users. The study showed there were people who used drugs on a regular and occasional basis without becoming physically dependent upon them. In many cases this usage seemed to be a rational choice to obtain a specific end, though some drug-takers in the second group did appear to be psychiatrically disturbed.

2 To observe the effects of drug-taking. The difficulties of doing this have already been discussed. The only point worth elaborating is that there are many accounts in the literature of subjects who committed dangerous acts while under the influence of LSD. In this study the observer saw four people taking LSD and talked to two others just after they had finished their first trip and in none of the cases did there appear to be any maleffects from these experiences.

3 To discover reasons why subjects took drugs. Whereas most of the reasons given appeared to be in line with those previously reported, e.g. for 'kicks', the use of LSD as a stimulant did not seem to have been recorded.

4 To discover possible hypotheses about differences between those who took drugs and those who didn't. The first group seemed to suggest that environmental factors were important in that if one moved in particular circles it would have been very difficult not to take drugs. However, in the second study where drugs were also freely available many people did not appear to take them. It may have been that they had tried them and disliked their effects, or it may have been that only the more psychiatrically disturbed members took drugs on a regular basis. What seemed to be important were the attitudes that one held towards drug-taking: members of the first group saw drugs as a necessary way of life whereas the members of the second group, who did not take drugs, saw no need for them, felt they were dangerous and that only disturbed people would take them. Another point which did seem worth following up was that some of the members of the second group, who did take drugs, appeared to come from troubled family backgrounds.

5 To gain information about the attitudes that were held about life and drugs. This in fact was obtained, i.e. the paranoic feeling about police, the rejection of the middle-class values of 'security' and 'respectability', etc.

6 To become familiar with the drug culture. This was also achieved except for the environment of the heroin addict.

Conclusion

The two studies made a valuable contribution towards the planning of the research, the hypotheses to be examined and the content of the questionnaires used.

5 The hypotheses

Nearly all the sources from which the hypotheses are derived have been discussed in the preceding chapters. The only exception is the pilot study, and, as its results do not alter the range of variables that other sources had suggested were important, its discussion has been left till the next chapter.

All the information on drug-taking that has so far been considered has indicated that drug-taking is multidetermined. By this it is meant that no one theory or environmental factor can account for why some people take drugs while others do not. Many factors are important in determining who takes drugs and the relevance of each of these factors might well vary from individual to individual. Many workers in the field support the idea that drug-taking is a multidetermined phenomenon:

SCHER (177:540): My own guess would be that a combination of availability, peer group enticement, the palling of socially acceptable directions and often an intensive urge for discovering and extending the limits of individual sensitivity and possibilities initiates many youngsters into early drug-taking experiences.

FORT (81:134): [Drugs can be used] ... as a food ... as a means of relieving tension, boredom and subsistence problems, for celebrating or socialising, as a means of obtaining temporary euphoria or escape, absence of alternative leisure time pursuits, sexual attitudes and beliefs, impaired social integration ... the influence of outside cultures or conformity to the mores of sub-cultures.

DAVIES (62:2–3): Drug-taking among these young people is apt to spread in the same way in which an infectious epidemic disease may spread, that is by contact with affected individuals. It may also spread as a consequence of the social and cultural attitudes of groups of young persons. It has already been observed that there must be deeper causes within the fabric of society leading to this phenomenon, for such centres of 'illicit' drug-taking arise among the youthful and teenage population ... without dis-

cernible contact with known centres of sources of supply . . .
(62:14). Broadly, therefore, it may be said that those who find life
too hard . . . may resort to drugs without benefit of medical advice.
To this group of people must be added the curious and adventur-
ous . . . finally there are those who take drugs in protest against
society.

HILTON (106) [on cannabis use among university students]:
'The user is made to feel part of an ingroup in that he is sharing
with others a forbidden pleasure and gains security from this. . . .
Many highly intelligent students find their courses uninteresting
and disappointing and lectures dull and uninspiring and therefore
revert to the drug as a result of their frustration. . . . In some cases
the impersonal atmosphere of a university, in which many people
are superficially known, but very few really close relationships
are formed, may breed intense insecurity and so lead the individual
to become a member of a group taking drugs merely for the social
satisfaction that it offers. In some cases the drug is taken out of
interest and curiosity as to its effects, or alternatively because it
provides a pleasant experience, which the individual enjoys, and
sees no reason to discontinue. Most students, however, seem to
regulate their use of hashish to once or twice a week at the most,
on finding that otherwise the drug interferes with their work, by
making them lethargic and unconcerned about it.
   Other reasons why marijuana is used include boredom,
curiosity, bravado, relief from fatigue, worry and strain, the
search for a new experience, as an escape from the problems of
everday life, insecurity, ignorance, the seeking of false courage,
glamour and social pressure. Often the drug is taken only for a
short time to get over a difficult period in one's life. The individual
may need to turn to fantasy to escape from problems which he
cannot face . . . it may be used as a reaction to an underlying
psychosis, or other psychological disorders.

As these quotations show, there are a diversity of reasons suggested
as to why young people take drugs. Some commentators go as
far as to suggest that there are no common threads at all: 'They
do not necessarily come from broken homes or homes in which
there is undue tension, or from poor or rich homes. Some are
intelligent, some are not and so on. Each individual case is
essentially an individual case, and there are no linking threads
or common factors' (210). Similarly the Addiction Research
Unit (132:1192) report that 'it is worth reiterating that there is
no such thing as a "typical junkie" '.

EDS

This variety of reasons was another determinant in deciding that this survey should try and test as wide a range of variables as possible. The reasons for drug-taking were grouped under the following headings: family and social class; availability; personality; drug knowledge; perceptual images; life style; attitudes to life; peer group relationships and environmental background.

Each of these groups will be considered in turn, the theoretical issues and experimental results will be discussed, and their relevance to drug-taking indicated. At the end of each discussion there will be listed the hypotheses which were tested in the main survey in each of these groups.

FAMILY AND SOCIAL CLASS

Social class

Social class is important as a variable because the different social classes are linked with different standards of living, and it is these differences which appear to be related to many social problems.

The evidence suggests that in this country drug-takers are likely to come from all social classes. It does, however, seem that some drugs might be used more frequently by people from one social class rather than those from another.

If one takes the figures for heroin addicts first the relevant findings are those by Hewetson and Ollendorf (105:110) where in a study of 100 addicts it was found that two were in social class 1, twenty-three were in class 2, fifty-two were in class 3 and twenty-three were in classes 4 and 5. Kaldegg (125:155), reporting on a highly selected addict population, said that they tended to come from both lower- and upper-middle-class homes. This finding is similar to Wilson-Kay's (210) report that his addict patients came from both rich and poor homes. One finding which contradicts this social class spread is that of the Addiction Research Unit (132:1190) who found that their subjects were evenly distributed between classes 1, 2 and 3 but none were in classes 4 and 5. It is interesting that this is the only study which includes a large number of non-institutionalised heroin users. In a final study Gillespie et al. (89:158) found that of sixteen heroin addicts, two were in social class 2, nine in class 3 and five in classes 4 and 5. This tendency for addicts in England to be spread across all social classes is in direct contrast to the situation in America where K. Cameron (35:145-7), quoting from a report,[1]

---

[1] Council of Mental Health of the A.M.A., *Report on Narcotic Addiction*.

says that 'addiction, particularly of youth, is found to be largely confined to very limited areas of the cities involved. These areas are the poorest in the cities and are characterised by the lowest incomes . . . most unstable family structures'. This observation is also reported by Finestone (77).

There is much less evidence, specially in this country, in connection with the social class backgrounds of users in the other drug categories. The two participant observation studies suggested that the members of the first group tended to come from middle and upper classes while members of the second group came primarily from the lower classes. This suggests that social class may not be as important a factor in drug use in England as in America. However, further information was obviously required before any firm conclusion could be drawn. As the findings also seemed to suggest that there might possibly be social class differences in the type of drug used it seemed worth while to include questions on social class in this survey.

The specific hypotheses explored were:

1 The lower the social class of the school childrens' families the more likely they are to have taken drugs (A 33, 34).[1]

2 The lower school children perceive their social class to be, the more likely they are to take drugs (A 38).

Family

There are many theories which attach importance to the influence of family relationships upon subsequent behaviour. They nearly all derive from the Freudian thesis which claims that a poor solution to the Oedipal situation results in a lack of identification with an appropriate father figure, with a subsequent malfunctioning of the superego. There have been many derivations stressing the importance of there being a male figure for the child to identify with. On the maternal side, the main work is Bowlby's (25) thesis of maternal deprivation. This says that if a child is separated for any length of time from its mother there will be detrimental effects on the child's later development. At the adolescent level of development it can be argued that the less identification that a child has with its family the more likely it is that the child will adopt the norms of his or her peer group as referents and the greater the likelihood therefore of the environment outside the

---

[1] The numbers in brackets refer to the questions in the questionnaire which test this hypothesis, see Appendix D, p. 182.

family influencing the child's behaviour. Evidence for this comes
from Schofield's (178:216) work where he found for example that
the more sexually experienced girls had greater antipathy to
family loyalty and dislike of adult interference than had less
sexually experienced girls.

There is a large amount of agreement among research workers
that the incidence of delinquency in general and drug-taking in
particular is related to poor family relationships. As regards the
general studies West (203:70) reports a project by Carr-Saunders
on nearly 2000 schoolboy offenders where delinquent and non-
delinquent boys from the same school were compared and it was
found that the proportion of delinquent cases in which one or
other of the natural parents was missing was approaching to
double that of the control group. Another study from West
(203:165–6), is that of Glueck, where 500 delinquents and their
controls were compared and it was found that the following
points, at the age of 6, best predicted future delinquency: degree
of discipline by father, supervision by mother, affection from
father, affection from mother and cohesiveness of the family.
Schofield (178:144) also found that the better girls got on with
their mother and father the less likely they were to be sexually
experienced and that boys who did not get on with their mother
were more likely to be sexually experienced. In another study in
West (203:162), McCord and McCord found, taking both the
degree of paternal and maternal affection into account, that among
the offspring of the worst parents, 81 per cent had been convicted
of some offence compared to only 28 per cent of the offspring from
the best parents.

A number of studies of American heroin addicts have shown
that family relationships appear to play an important part in
the specific deviance problem of drug-taking. Einstein (72:96)
quotes a study by Alksne[1] which reports that in 50 per cent of
drug addicts a significant male figure was missing by the time the
addict was 11 years old. Chein et al. (45:273–4) found that 'in
almost all the addict families, there was a disturbed relationship
between the parents . . . one theme was almost invariably the
same—the absence of a warm relationship with a father figure
with whom the boy could identify'. Fort (80:81) similarly says
that a lot of addicts lack a father figure, while a report on drug
addiction (160:188) found that broken homes was one of the

[1] Alksne, H. (1959). A follow up of treated adolescent narcotic users.
Report prepared for the N.Y. State Inter. Dept Health Resources Bureau
Board, October 1959

reasons for addiction. Laskowitz (135:70) similarly reports that addicts are overpampered while Nylander (161:51) found that Swedish chronic thinner addicts usually came from severely emotionally disturbed homes.

In connection with English addicts the Addiction Research Unit (132:1190) found that in nine out of thirty-five cases the parents of heroin drug users were either divorced, separated or not both alive.

Less is known about the non-addict drug-taking population. Scott and Willcox (180: 17) found that the more severe drug-takers (pep pills) were overdependent upon their parents and came from grossly unfavourable home backgrounds.

This review has indicated that a number of factors to do with family relationships, for example loss of a parent, are related to the incidence of drug-taking. As these factors also appeared to be common to many forms of deviance it would not be expected that they would differentiate drug-trakers from other deviants. However, as these factors seemed to be important in differentiating deviants in general, and drug-takers in particular, from non-deviants, it seemed to be essential to include them.

Five hypotheses were finally formulated to test the significance of these factors. They were:

3 The less close school children perceive themselves to have been to their fathers from childhood onwards the more likely they are to take drugs (B 2, 9, 17, 22, 28).

4 The closer a male school child feels to his mother and the more distant a female school child feels to her mother, the more likely they are to take drugs (B 5, 13, 19, 21, 32).

5 The greater the degree of parental control the less likely school children are to take drugs (B 4, 6, 11, 24, 29, 30, 33).

6 The greater the degree of parental leniency the more likely school children are to take drugs (B 8, 10, 15, 23, 31).

7 The less privacy school children have at home the more likely they are to take drugs (A 5, 6, 7).

AVAILABILITY

The most obvious hypothesis is that the more drug-takers a person knows the more likely is it that he or she will turn to drug-taking. If one now adds reference group theory to this hypothesis then it becomes possible to specify more clearly under which conditions a person is likely to follow the example set by others. Reference group theory would argue that if those who took the drugs were members of the same group from which an individual took his norms of behaviour, then the individual would be more likely to take drugs than if the drug-taking group were merely peer group members. Therefore one can be more specific in one's hypothesis and contend that if the drug-takers a person knows are also members of his reference group then he will be more likely to take drugs than if they were not.

The data on availability suggests that the hypothesis mentioned above is realistic. As regards the American heroin addiction problem Fort (80:78) reports that most addicts are introduced by those already on the habit, as does Isbell (117:18).

The position is similar in England. Both the Addiction Research Unit (132:1192) and Linken (146) report that drug-taking spreads through already existing friendship patterns. As regards drugs other than heroin, there were attempts during the first participant observation study to proselytise friends to the enjoyment of drugs.

If it is the case that availability leads to an increased likelihood of the taking of drugs, just how available are drugs? Wilson and Linken (209) claim that cannabis is available in all large cities. The Brain Committee (102:12) noted the availability of drugs in parts of London: 'Witnesses have told us that there are numerous clubs, many in the West End of London, enjoying a vogue among young people . . . in such places it is known that some young people have indulged in stimulant drugs of the amphetamine type.' The second participant observation study would indicate that this still holds true. The survey of headmasters similarly reports that 'it is unfortunately true that the drugs are available in clubs, coffee bars, dance halls, youth clubs, etc., all over the area'.

It appeared, therefore, that the availability of drugs, particularly within one's friendship or reference group, might well be one reason in determining whether a person took drugs or not and what type of drugs he would take. That this was likely to happen was shown by the fact that drugs were freely available in many areas that schoolboys would be likely to visit. The specific hypotheses tested were:

8 The more people school children know who have taken drugs the more likely they are to take drugs (A 20).

9 The more times school children have been in the company

of other boys or girls who have taken drugs the more likely
they are to take drugs (A 17).

DRUG KNOWLEDGE

There were two reasons why it appeared to be important to
measure drug knowledge. First, if one were to run an educational
programme it would be important to discover not only what
subjects did not know and what erroneous beliefs would have
to be corrected, but also to find out at what level such a programme would have to be pitched. The second reason was to
find out to what extent drug knowledge acted as a deterrent.
Previous work on attitude change had revealed the fact that
the relationship between knowledge and attitude change was
complex. This point will be discussed in more detail in later
chapters.

In the field of drug-taking it might have been expected that one
of the reasons why people took heroin was because they were not
aware of the dangers. At a first glance this seems to be the case.
Leech and Jordan (139:70), for example, say that many people
start taking drugs in ignorance, not knowing what the drugs are,
or what they are supposed to do or how many to take to get the
desired effect. Similarly a report on drug addiction (160:189) says
that ignorance and curiosity are two of the necessary ingredi-
ents for initiating drug use. Chein et al. (45:155) found that many
of the male users said that they had learnt nothing cautionary
about drug-use 'before' starting whereas 79 per cent of delinquent
non-users said that they had. The three points the non-users most
often mentioned against the use of heroin were: health, the cost
of the habit and resort to illegal activities and, thirdly, that the
drug would lead to a deterioration of character. However, in
almost complete contrast with female addicts, Chein et al.
(45:305) found that

> all the patients knew that heroin is illicit, habit-forming and
> possibly lethal (through an overdose), and they believed that
> heroin use is debilitating. However, they were also aware of
> its reputation as 'a good way to get high', that is they expected
> relaxing and comforting effects. Their first use clearly did not
> express ignorance, but rather disregard for what they knew
> about the long-range probabilities of harm and trouble in the
> quest for immediate pleasure.

Therefore knowledge about the dangers of heroin does not mean this will prevent people using heroin.

In the non-heroin field virtually nothing is known about the relationship between drug knowledge and usage. Linken (146) found that many of his subjects had some knowledge about drugs while Scher (177:541), referring to the American situation, says that few campus cannabis users switch to opiates because the students are aware of the dangers. This same respect for heroin was also present among members of the first participant observation study. Perhaps in these two instances the people might have had knowledge about the respective dangers of each of the drugs while in other cases people only had a general knowledge, such that when they had tried one drug and found it quite harmless they assumed all drugs were harmless.

Chein *et al.* (45:97–8) also found that drug knowledge was related to the degree of incidence in any one area. They found for example that in high drug areas all subjects, whether delinquent or not, had some degree of drug knowledge while in the low use drug areas only the delinquent group had this knowledge.

It appeared important to find out more about the relationship between drug knowledge and drug use both for purposes of future education and also for understanding what sort of knowledge appeared to be most effective and useful. The specific hypothesis tested was:

10 The more specific and accurate the drug knowledge school children have the more likely they are to take drugs (F 1–70).

PERCEPTUAL IMAGES

The perception that a person has of a drug-taker is important, because if a deterrent educational campaign were going to be run and if it were found that young people perceived drug-takers as being especially tough people, then this would be the image that such a campaign would have to destroy.

The relevance to education of the perception of drug-takers is pointed out by Davies (62:17) who writes: 'in schools, factories, and indeed any community of youth, the idea that drugs help a boy or girl to be braver, more successful or sexually more powerful should be replaced by a picture of the impairment of the attainment of these desired qualities'. What such a scale would do in this case would be in the first instance to establish that the picture Davies draws of how drugs are perceived, is in fact accurate.

A third reason for the use of perceptual scales is that it becomes possible to verify an observation by Schiff, reported in Chein *et al.* (45:191), where it is argued that narcotic users have too little self esteem to make the grade to adult status and therefore turn to drugs instead. This is in keeping with their observation (45:191–2) that it is the people who cannot make the transition from teenage gangs to respectable adulthood who are likely to turn to drugs.

To look at these three points three scales were used: One measuring perception of the self, one that of the ideal self and the last one that of drug-takers.

The specific hypotheses tested were:

11 The greater the similarity between the perception of the ideal self and that of the drug-takers, the more likely one is to take drugs (E, H).

12 The greater the similarity between the self and the ideal self and the greater the discrepancy with the perception of the drug-taker the less likely one is to take drugs (D, E, H).

13 The greater the similarity between the perception of the self and the perception of the drug-taker the more likely one is to take drugs (D, H).

LIFE STYLE

Delinquency

The main question is whether a person is more likely to take drugs if he or she is already a delinquent, i.e. to what extent is drug-taking among young people simply one facet of a general delinquency syndrome? The evidence indicates first, that while some delinquents take drugs by no means all do; secondly, that many apprehended drug-takers have had a prior history of delinquency; and thirdly, that there are many drug-takers who are not delinquent, or at least have not been apprehended for it.

In looking at the data on the first point Scott and Willcox (180:12) in a study of boys and girls at a remand home found that 17 per cent of boys and 20 per cent of girls had recently taken amphetamines.

The second point was that many drug-takers have a prior history of delinquency. As regards the figures for American heroin addicts Laskowitz (135:67) reports a study by Alksne who found that 70 per cent of addicts committed to Riverside hospital had a history of one or more offences. This pattern of crime and addiction in America might well be a result of the culture's legal attitude to heroin use; however, the few available English figures tend to repeat the pattern even though there is not the same necessity here for addict to turn to crime.

It must be pointed out that most of the data refers to heroin addiction and it may well be that offenders in other drug categories do not have such a long history in delinquency. Secondly, very little is known about the delinquency record of non-institutionalised addicts. The Addiction Research Unit (132:1191) found for example that only three out of thirty-one subjects had been convicted of offences before using any drugs at all. Thirdly, once a person has been in trouble with the police he is much more likely to be in trouble with them again because he will be known to the police as someone with a record. Therefore drug-takers with a delinquency record are much more likely to be apprehended than those with a clean record. Kaldegg (125:155), referring to hospitalised rather than imprisoned addicts, says that few addicts commit offences other than drug offences. The point is that whereas many institutionalised addicts have a history of delinquency this does not necessarily apply to non-institutionalised addicts nor to drug-takers in other categories.

In looking at the third point, that there are many drug-takers who have no delinquency record, data is hard to find. In the two participant observation studies, with particular reference to the first, the majority of the poeple observed had no delinquency record to the knowledge of the observer. Similarly to the extent that estimates like Wilson and Linken's (209), that 10 per cent of university students use drugs, are correct, one can assume that not all of these will have had a delinquency record.

It appears, therefore, that drug-taking involves members of the community who are not in other ways delinquent. It does, however, also appear that some delinquents do take drugs either because their way of life brings them into contact with drugs or because in some sub-cultures drug-taking is part of the delinquent norm. It did, therefore, seem to be a point in need of further evidence and the specific hypotheses tested were:

14 If school children have been in trouble with the police they are more likely to have taken drugs (A 9, 10).

15 The more more delinquent friends school children have the more likely they are to take drugs (A 11).

Education and job aspirations

One factor which appeared to be characteristic of a number of heroin addicts and therefore worthy of further scrutiny was that addicts appeared to be underachievers in both educational and vocational fields. This underachieving was noticeable before the person started to use heroin and was not therefore a result of the addiction process. Empirically the Addiction Research Unit (132:1190) found that nineteen of the addicts had failed to complete a course either at school or in further part- or full-time education, and that those who held jobs worked in positions below those one would expect given their background. Hewetson and Ollendorf (105:110) in a study of 100 addicts found forty-eight had never taken any examination and twenty were near illiterate. In America Finestone (77:151–2) claims that few addicts ever finish high school.

Though there is no similar data available for non-heroin-users underachievement seemed to be a factor worth following up, especially as McKennell and Bynner (153:36) found that smokers were more often to be found among the low achievement groups. The particular hypotheses tested were:

16 The younger a person leaves school the more likely he is to take drugs (A 1).

17 The more upwardly mobile school children are in their job aspirations the less likely they are to take drugs (A 33–6).

Leisure pursuits

We have already seen that drugs are freely available in the coffee bars, dance halls, etc., of many English towns. Does it therefore follow that people with a pattern of leisure pursuits which includes visiting these types of places will be more likely to take drugs than people with a different pattern? A second point following from this is that, if this is the case, are drugs taken because these people are bored?

The evidence for the first point comes first from the survey of headmasters which, reporting on seventy-four juveniles who had appeared on drug offences, found that most were arrested in the early hours of the morning, during a weekend in the vicinity of clubs and coffee bars. The report goes on to say that one reason why these people take pep pills is that as transport stops so early they need to take the pills to be able to stay awake and dance in clubs all night. The second participant observation study found exactly the same thing occurring. Connell (54:26) has also noted that pep pills are taken mainly over weekends. Of these pep pill-takers Bewley (18:6) says:

> Many of them would appear to be adolescents who a few years ago would have been getting drunk on a Saturday night and who now merely take a number of amphetamines in order to remain 'high' while at parties or in groups with other users. It is probably that large numbers of adolescents experiment with these drugs and, at a later date, abandon them and settle down to a more stable, better adjusted adult life. The first participant observation study indicated that cannabis and LSD could be used for similar functional reasons.

As regards the second point, that of boredom, Louria (149:75) talking about American drug-taking says that 'a major problem in regard to drug abuse is that too many young people have too much time on their hands'. Chein *et al.* (45:146) substantiate this for they found that the life style of future users included 'less use of libraries, extracurricular activities and some of the less common leisure activities than did the control group . . . the users often mentioned going to movies, hanging around candy stores; goofing off'. Similarly, Leech and Jordan (139:61) in this country say that those who indulge in occasional pill-taking and cannabis smoking tend to be young people 'who are without any particular direction or aim in life, who may well be utterly bored with their monotonous existence at home, at school or at work'.

It therefore appeared that both the type and the range of activities indulged in might be an important indicator of whether a person would be likely to take drugs or not. The specific hypotheses tested were:

18 The more times school children go to parties, coffee bars, pubs, Soho or dances, rather than participating in alternative activities, the more likely they are to take drugs (A 12).

19 The worse school children feel they have done at school the more likely they are to take drugs (A 8).

20 Children who are about to leave school are more likely to take drugs than other school children (A 2).

21 The more school children smoke the more likely they are to take drugs (A 24).

22 The more school children drink alcohol the more likely they are to take drugs (A 30–1).

23 The more school children save money the less likely they are to take drugs (A 15).

ATTITUDES TO LIFE AND VALUES HELD

To what extent does the available data support the notion that drug taking is part of a wider rejection of the conventional society? Leech and Jordan (139:61) obviously believe that this is the case:

> Very often the potential addict sees all too clearly the mess around him in his own life, the violence and destruction in society which shows itself in everyday living, and consciously or unconsciously chooses self-destruction rather than take part in the society around him whose values disgust him.

A. K. Cohen (48:88–91) lists the conventional middle-class ethics as being: ambition, individual responsibility, cultivation and possession of skills, worldly ascetism, a readiness to postpone immediate gratification, rationality, cultivation of manners, courtesy and persuasibility, control of physical aggression and violence and respect for property.

The rejection of these values seems also to be a characteristic of the addict's ideology because according to Kaldegg (125:155) the addict feels that this is a bad, rotten world in which we can only find a form of personal existence.

This rejection of conventional values seems to apply also to drug users of other categories. Leech (138: para. 11), for example, says 'these "trippers" are generally highly intelligent and sensitive people and some would say that they obtain direct spiritual enlightenment through use of the drug'. Members of the first participant observation study similarly stressed the importance of the discovery and expression of the self in a creative manner in place of the aims of the conventional society.

It also seemed interesting to find out to what extent drug-takers would be similar to the sexually experienced boys in Schofield's study (178:208) who tended to oppose restrictions on their behaviour and accepted the idea 'that teenagers are alienated from the adult world and that nothing in life is as important as enjoyment'. Therefore the rejection of conventional norms did appear to be a factor which might play a part in determining whether a person took drugs or not. The specific hypotheses tested were:

24 The more a school leaver repudiates middle-class norms the more likely he is to take drugs (C 1–17).

25 The more emphasis a school leaver places upon materialistic as against other life goals the more likely he is to take drugs (C).

ATTITUDES TO DRUGS

To what extent does the likelihood of holding favourable attitudes towards the taking of drugs increase the probability of someone taking drugs. The only available evidence comes from Chein *et al.*, who found firstly (45:12), that in high drug areas there was a marked connection between delinquency orientation and favourable attitudes to narcotics. Secondly (45:103), they found that the most tolerant attitudes to drugs existed among boys in the highest drug use area, and thirdly (45:145), they found that non-drug-takers all said that their friends who mattered all held negative attitudes towards drugs.

Though these findings do indicate that drug use is related to attitudes towards drugs there is no comparable study in this country. The only survey on this topic was carried out by the *Melody Maker* (155) who asked one hundred of its readers about drugs after Paul McCartney had admitted to taking LSD. There therefore appeared to be a need for such a study. The specific hypothesis tested was:

26 The more favourable the attitudes towards drug-taking that school children hold the more likely they are to take drugs (G).

PEER GROUP RELATIONSHIPS

We have seen in the discussion on 'availability' that if drugs are present within a group which serves as a reference group for an individual it is reasonable to hypothesise that he might be tempted to follow the example set by them. This section will take a further look at the data which suggests first, that not only is there a motivation for a person to 'do right' in the eyes of his peers but there is also pressure by them on him; and secondly, that in other instances it might be the individual who does not belong to a group who is most likely to take drugs.

In connection with the first point Leech and Jordan (139:71) write: 'If the individual wants to keep going with the group and the group takes pills or smokes "pot", the individual often gives in to the majority even though it may be against his personal scruples.' Likewise Connell (54:24) reports 'teenagers take drugs to be with it', while an already mentioned study by the Addiction Research Unit (132:1192) has shown that drug-taking often spreads through friendship patterns.

Reports from America are similar. Harms (99:3) gives the following as reasons why young people take drugs: (i) give it a try, (ii) because others did it, (iii) to be a good sport in the eyes of peers, (iv) desire to be a hero and (v) part of group membership. Winick (211:27) similarly says that drug-taking sometimes serves as an entry to a group. Krug *et al.* (133:43) in reference to the abuse of commercial solvents says that the child who discovers the habit in his group will often become the source of supply and the 'leader' in trying to persuade others to try it.

Therefore if one's reference group takes drugs it becomes important for an individual to follow suit, not only to gain admission to the group but also to retain group membership. There also appears to be pressure from within the group to covert non-taking members. This is probably related to security considerations because if everyone commits the illegal act then no one is likely to turn informer.

However, in some cases it is the individual who cannot form group relationships who is most likely to take drugs. This observation is made by Finestone (77:150) and by Knapp (131:427) who found that amphetamine addicts were isolated individuals.

Therefore group membership seemed important to follow up, because if one's reference group took drugs there was an increased likelihood that the individual would. It was therefore important first to establish whether a person's reference group consisted of his peers or of his elders. The American evidence suggested that the poorer the area the greater the likelihood that a person's reference group would consist of his peers and, as Finestone (77:147) points out, these areas in America have the highest drug rates. One would expect therefore in this country that a peer group would be an important factor to the extent that it functioned as a reference group for an individual, and whether it had drug-taking as a norm of behaviour. The specific hypotheses tested were:

27 The more anxious school children are about peer group relationships the more likely they are to take drugs (B 1, 7, 12, 16, 21, 25).

28 The longer school children spend with their peer group the more likely they are to take drugs (A 12c, l,/n, o, and A 13).

29 The more school children use a peer rather than an adult as a confidant the more likely they are to take drugs (A 37).

PERSONALITY

Most studies agree that addicts have disturbed personalities, but there is disagreement as to the extent to which this existed before the onset of addiction and to what extent the disturbance occurred after the start of the addictive process. D. C. Cameron (34:314) quotes a report[1] which says that, the psychiatric conditions preceded and played an important part in the genesis of addiction. Similarly in England, Willis (208:222), after looking at the life style of addicts before they became addicted, concludes that 'heroin had merely intensified their assorted levels of maladjustment'. However, Scher (177:545) argues that personality disturbances may possibly occur after addiction and not before.

Given that addicts have inadequate personalities, what are its characteristics. The most catholic description is given by Fort (81:134–5) about American addicts when he says:

From a psychological viewpoint the drug abuser has been described . . . as passive, overdependent, inadequate, immature, intolerant of frustration or stress, self destructive and anxious about sexual and aggressive drives. Freudian psycho-analysts have written on the subject in terms of latent homosexuality or fixation at, or regression to, an infantile (usually oral) level of psychosexual development due to having an overindulgent mother and an inadequate father.

Frankau (82:1377–8) describes a sample of thirty-six English heroin addicts as 'immature, inadequate and unstable . . . low threshold for pain . . . (in need of) immediate gratification . . . no tolerance of criticism . . . untruthful'. Similar descriptions are

---

[1] The Council on Mental Health, A.M.A., *Report on Narcotic Addiction*.

given by Louria (149:13) and by Chein *et al.* (45:255) who conclude that 'the potential male addict suffers from (i) a weak ego structure, (ii) defective superego functioning, and (iii) inadequate masculine identification'.

Some light is thrown on the matter of whether personality disturbances preceded addiction or not by looking at people who take drugs other than heroin. The evidence here suggests that the more seriously disturbed are likely to become the heavier abusers and are more likely to end up in institutions. For example, Wilson and Linken (209) say:

> The available evidence suggests that those members of the modern student body and of the adolescent age group who are immature, emotionally undeveloped or mentally unstable are the ones who are predisposed to seek the escape from reality and relief from the strains and stresses of adolescence and university and college demands.

Linken (146) in his study of venereal patients found that 16 per cent of those who took drugs had previously received psychiatric treatment. Davies (62:10) similarly comments that adolescents who are either neurotic or inadequate are at risk to becoming dependent. Similarly very aggressive adolescents may find that 'drugs help them to show their feelings of aggression with even less inhibition than is usual for them'. Some more evidence comes from Scott and Willcox (180:17) who found that regular takers showed a lack of self confidence in personal relationships and behave in a fearful, self-doubting, sometimes persecuted manner.

These findings indicate that regular takers are likely to be disturbed people, and if these are the subjects who escalate to heroin then this would imply that the disturbances existed before the onset of addiction. It would not, however, show whether they existed before any drug-taking behaviour. That it might be the case that they did not is shown by the fact that the occasional drug-takers do not necessarily appear to be very disturbed individuals. This might either mean that regular and occasional drug users have different personality characteristics, or it might mean that as drug-taking increases there is a corresponding decrease in the level of personality functioning.

The data on occasional users comes first from Scott and Willcox (180:20–21) who report that the occasional users who took drugs only at weekends had no unsatisfactory personality disorders as judged by a capacity to make personal relationships with both

FDS

sexes. Holden (108:33) similarly divides London's West End teenagers into two sorts. The hard core are those who started off as weekend users and escalated, who have no steady jobs, and many of whom are delinquents. The second group are the occasional users who are

> relatively stable and are merely going through a phase of adolescent rebellion or experimentation in the course of a search for their own identity. Many of these youngsters experiment with drugs, mostly marijuana and amphetamines in the same kind of way as they experiment with alcohol. The great majority abandon both drugs and alcohol after a short time as 'not worth it'.

It seems, therefore, that occasional users are not necessarily disturbed, those who are regular users and who escalate appear to be. It may well be that these people are also the most delinquent. A study on Borstal subjects (10) found no personality differences between subjects who admitted taking drugs and those who said they had not used drugs.

As personality only appeared to be important in differentiating regular from occasional drug users it seemed unlikely that it would be particularly important in a study of school children where those who took drugs were only likely to be occasional users. However, it was decided to include a personality scale in case it was possible to discriminate between children in their degree of drug use. As Chein et al. (45:255) had found American heroin addicts had a 'weak ego structure' it was decided to concentrate upon this aspect of personality. The specific hypothesis tested was:

30 The greater the ego strength school children have the less likely they are to take drugs (B).

PART TWO

Methodology

6 Design of the research

RESEARCH DESIGN

'*A cross sectional design cannot tell us anything about cause-and-effect relationships, it can only provide us with information about correlates. In an effort to overcome this, longitudinal or before-and-after designs have been developed*' (Oppenheim 224:16).

The original intention of this survey was to employ a longitudinal design. Specifically the plan was to take children in their last or second last year at school and follow them up a year or more later. The advantage of this design would have been that it would have enabled one to be sure which, of any differences found between drug-takers and non-drug-takers, had pre-existed the onset of drug-taking and might therefore have been causal factors. The assumption was that by taking the children in their last or second last year at school a sample would have been obtained in which comparatively few subjects had taken drugs. During the subsequent year it was hoped that a number of the subjects would have tried drugs and it would then have been possible to have compared these subjects on a number of variables with those who, during the same period of time, had not tried drugs. If any differences had then been found, dependent on the extent to which it was possible to control other factors, it would have been viable to say that these differences were probably contributing factors as to why some subjects took drugs and others did not.

After consideration it proved impossible to employ a longitudinal design. The idea of taking children in their last year at school and following them up a year or so later had to be abandoned because of the time, facilities and expense that this would have involved, for instance in the training of a panel of interviewers. Even if this idea had been utilised it would have run into the problem that once out of school subjects would have branched into different careers, friendship groups, and leisure pursuits. This would have made it difficult to know to what extent any differences found between drug-takers and non-drug-takers were due to these factors and to what extent they were due to the taking of drugs.

The second alternative considered was to take children in their penultimate year at school and then follow them up a year later. This plan, though it would have had the advantage of standardising the environment of the subjects, had also to be rejected, for two reasons. First, it was unlikely that a sufficiently large number of subjects would begin taking drugs during their last year at school to be able to make a significant comparison possible.[1] The second reason was the problem of confidentiality. Because drug-taking is an illegal activity it was felt that if the children knew that they could be identified they would be less likely to tell the truth.[2] The problem was that if a follow up was being done it was essential for the investigator to be able to identify which child had filled in which questionnaire. There are of course various methods of identifying questionnaires without the child knowing it, such as by getting the child to fill in his form name and date of birth and then checking these against the school records. However, in this case it was felt that given the problem of small numbers of probable drug-takers and the unlikelihood of the schools' cooperation in the identification of the questionnaires, such a deception would not be warranted.

A different approach would have been to use a factorial design 'whose particular function is to disentangle complex sets of inter-relationships' (Oppenheim 224:13). As it appeared that many factors contributed to the likelihood of drug-taking this design would have been appropriate as it would have enabled one to discover to what extent each factor contributed. In a factorial design a cell is formed for each possible combination of factors and then each cell is compared with the others to see if any significant differences occur. The difficulty with this design is pointed out by Oppenheim (224:14), who (assuming that five variables had been decided on as being of particular importance for drug-taking), says: 'let us assume that we have ten age divisions, seven socioeconomic grades, and five family size groupings, while sex and urban/rural are dichotomies. This would give us a design

---

[1] The results of this survey in fact supported this assumption.

[2] In the comments on the back of the questionnaire some children commented that it was only because they believed the questionnaire to be anonymous that they answered truthfully.

containing 10 × 7 × 5 × 2 × 2 = 1400 (cells), which, even at no more than ten cases per cell would require 14,000 children.' Not only was any number of children approaching this out of reach on administrative grounds but it was extremely unlikely that 14,000 or so school children could have been found who took drugs, without combing a vast quantity of schools.

Another approach could have been to undertake a purely descriptive survey for the purpose of obtaining a reliable estimate of the number of children who took drugs in London for example. This would have meant drawing some sort of random sample of school children from a number of London boroughs, stratifying for type of school. This was not done for three reasons. First, because the survey was primarily interested in differences between drug-takers and non-drug-takers and only secondarily in obtaining an estimate of the numbers who took drugs. Secondly, it was beyond the scope of this survey to be able to provide a sample large enough to be representative of anything but one or two educational districts. Thirdly, a representative sample depends upon the cooperation of all the selected schools and children. This did not appear to be an assumption that one could make about this topic, and in fact in the second part of the sample, when an attempt was made to draw a representative sample of the schools in one educational district, only three of the six headmasters approached agreed to cooperate.

The design finally chosen was an analytical cross-sectional design. Analytical refers to the fact that the survey is 'set up specifically to explore the relationships between particular variables' (Oppenheim 224:9) rather than simply to count numbers as in a descriptive survey. Cross-sectional refers to the fact that all of the subjects are tested at one time. This, as was pointed out at the beginning of this section, normally means that if any differences are found between the experimental and the control group (in this case drug-takers and non-drug-takers) it is difficult to know whether these differences are due to the drug-taking or whether they existed before the drug-taking started, when, if so, they well might be causal factors. This criticism is not so relevant where the subjects are still at school, because it is unlikely that the drug-taking will be of sufficient length or seriousness to have had any significant effect on the individual's behaviour. It is therefore likely that any differences found between drug-takers and non-drug-takers are also likely to have existed before the drug-taking began and might therefore be treated as possible causal factors.

Within the framework of this design schools were chosen on

the likelihood of their having a high percentage of drug-takers. This served two purposes. First, as the primary aim of the survey was to compare drug-takers with non-drug-takers, it seemed sensible to try to maximise the number of drug-takers. Second, as it was not possible to obtain a representative sample the best alternative appeared to be to choose schools with the highest suspected number of drug-takers in the district. This would enable one to argue that if anything the problem was unlikely to be any worse in any of the other schools in the district and from this one could therefore obtain a rough estimate of the maximum number of school children taking drugs in any one district.

Within any survey design the experimenter is concerned with four types of variables. First, there is the dependent variable. This is the one the survey primarily deals with, in this case, whether someone takes drugs or not. The second type covers the independent variables, whose effect on the dependent variable the experimenter is trying to find. In this case they are factors like personality, life style, etc. The third group contains the controlled variables. Here the experimenter tries to prevent factors other than the independent ones from affecting the dependent variable. For example, if the survey had been conducted over a period of many months, and if those who had taken drugs were all found in the later stages, then one would not have known whether differences between drug-takers and non-drug-takers were due to those hypothesised or to the difference in time when they participated in the survey. To prevent this happening the experimenter 'controls' these factors. He can do this by either holding them constant, that is to say surveying all the sample at one time, or he can use matching, that is each drug-taker would be 'matched' with a control subject who had participated in the survey at the same time. In this case both methods were used. For example, the whole survey was completed within three months, and all of the drug-takers were matched with a control group on the factors of sex, age, school and social class.

The final type of variable is the uncontrolled one: differences might be due to a factor which one had not realised was common to one group and not to the other. For example, if one had not controlled for age it might well have been that all drug-takers were three years older than the other subjects and that therefore any differences found would perhaps be due to the differential rather than to the factor of drug-taking. One way to avoid this happening is to carry out many cross-checks when tabulating the data. This was done in this survey.

In summary, therefore, a cross-sectional design was chosen within which a basic measure of control was obtained by matching the drug-takers with non-drug-takers on a number of variables.

QUESTIONNAIRES *V*. INTERVIEWS

In the preliminary stages of the work, when the experimenter was trying to find out as much about the field as possible, interviews were carried out with many people working on the problem. These interviews were completely unstructured and no attempt was made to standardise the information obtained in them. However, in the main part of the survey, where standardisation was necessary, a decision had to be made as to whether some form of structured interview as used by Schofield (178) or whether a series of group administered questionnaires as used in the Government Social Survey (95) study of cigarette smoking would be the best method to obtain the data.

Both approaches had their respective advantages and dis-advantages. According to Jahoda, Deutsch and Cook (221:157–8) the general advantages of the interview are that they are more flexible, they enable probing to find a subject's 'true' meaning, they are better for taboo information and overcome problems of illiteracy. Among their other advantages, according to Oppenheim (224:31), are that they enable rapport to be built up and they allow a greater richness of material to be obtained. Questionnaires also have their advantages. These are, that they can be given to a group, they are simple to administer and quick to analyse, and their impersonality ensures a form of standardisation. They are also cheaper and require fewer staff.

On the other hand there are the disadvantages to consider. Interviews are very costly, they involve the training of staff, they are time consuming, there is often difficulty in the coding of answers and finally there is the problem of unreliability arising because of interviewer variability in approach and the degree of rapport established. The disadvantages of questionnaires are that they require more planning and piloting, and they presume a degree of literacy from the subjects.

As regards the problem of drug-taking in particular the strongest argument for using interviews for at least part of the survey is that one is dealing with a taboo subject. The assumption is that because drug-taking is an illegal activity, subjects are either likely to deny existent drug experiences or to boast about drug-taking experiences that have not occurred. The advantage of an interview is that one can challenge statements about drug-taking episodes and probe for further information. This was similar to the method used by Kinsey (223) in his study of the sexual behaviour of the American population.

In this case interviews would have involved a financial and time expenditure which was not available. It was therefore essential to use questionnaires not only for this reason but also because the group testing, which the questionnaires permitted, was the simplest to work with, within the school system. Another advantage of using questionnaires was that, except possibly for the actual question about drug-taking, the rest of the information concerning attitudes, or drug knowledge, was best collected in this form both for the testing of hypotheses and for the analysis of the data in terms of problems of standardisation, reliability, coding and so on. A final reason for using questionnaires was that if a series of interviews are carried out within a school word soon gets around as to the purpose of the interview and this creates a bias.

There still remained the problem of dealing with a taboo topic. This was dealt with in two ways. First, to overcome the problem that people were unlikely to admit to an illegal and taboo activity it was decided to disguise the fact that this questionnaire was aimed primarily at drug-taking. Among the steps taken to do this were firstly, that the school children were told that the questionnaire was aimed at finding out about problems in general.[1] Secondly, the questionnaire was so designed that in the first half of it there were only three questions on drug-taking and these were sand-wiched between questions on cigarette and alcohol consumption. This ruse seemed to be successful as less than 3 per cent of the children, as taken by their comments written on the back of their questionnaires when they had finished, worked out what the questionnaire was really after. This therefore went some way to answer the first part of the problem. The second point was to overcome the fact that subjects might be boasting. This was done by having internal checks within the questionnaire. For example, if someone said that he took drugs frequently then he would also have to have said that he knew other people who took drugs.

The other disadvantages of questionnaires, those of literacy and the amount of planning and piloting required, do not apply in this case. This is first, because all the children sampled were

---

just about to leave school and a minimum standard of literacy could therefore be assumed. Secondly, the type of questions asked demanded an intensive degree of piloting and this therefore was a necessity and not a disadvantage.

Therefore, though unstructured interviews were used in the initial stages of the work it was decided on the grounds of cost, group testing, appropriateness to the information required, time and analysis that questionnaires would be used to elicit the main part of the data.

Though it had been decided to use questionnaires a decision still had to be made as to how they should be administered. There were two alternatives. The first was to send the school sufficient questionnaires for all its school leavers, ask them to distribute them and either collect them oneself or have them returned directly to the experimenter. The second approach was for the experimenter to administer the questionnaires to a group of subjects and collect them himself immediately they had finished.

The first approach was discarded for five reasons. The first was that if the school administration was concerned at any stage with the handling of the questionnaires the subjects might no longer believe in their anonymity. Secondly, there was no guarantee that all the questionnaires would be returned. Thirdly, there was no check as to whether the subject had completed the questionnaire on his own. Fourthly, on questions of knowledge the experimenter would not have known whether the subject had consulted authoritative texts or not. The fifth reason was that if subjects had too long a time to peruse the questionnaires it was likely that they would guess its purpose.

The second approach was therefore used. The influence of the school was reduced by the experimenter bringing in an outside team to administer the questionnaires and by the fact that where possible no teachers were present during the administration. All questionnaires were immediately collected. The main disadvantage of this approach was that it meant that children who were not present at school that day did not complete the questionnaires.

BASIC DESIGN OF THE QUESTIONNAIRE

There were two preliminary drafts of the questionnaire before the final version was arrived at. The first draft, designed at the beginning of the study, was solely concerned with determining how best to ask questions about drug-taking behaviour. This question-naire was given to members of a youth club, to a religious group and to students at the Institute of Criminology. This questionnaire proved to be particularly helpful in designing questions about drug-taking so that subjects realised that one was only interested in drugs taken illegally.

The second draft was the one used in the pilot study. In the light of the findings of this study changes were made with regard to the choice of items, question wordings, etc., but the basic form remained the same in the final version. This basic form con-sisted of nine sections, A–I. In the second sample tested in the main survey an additional section, J, was included.[1]

Section A

This section was concerned with finding out background informa-tion about the subjects and included questions for testing hypo-theses on the life style of subjects, availability of drugs, job aspirations, peer group relationships, social class and privacy. This section also included the crucial question on whether subjects took drugs or not. This was placed between questions on cigarette and alcohol consumption and the wording of questions was such that the question on drug-taking appeared to be no different from those on cigarette and alcohol consumption. The questions on cigarettes and alcohol served two purposes. They disguised the question on drugs, and they appeared to be useful questions to ask in their own right. For example, Schofield (178:176–8) had found that sexually experienced teenagers smoked more and had been to a pub more recently than sexually non-experienced teen-agers.

A number of studies contributed to the content and wording of questions. As regards leisure pursuits of teenagers a study referred to was one by Stewart (188:34) in 1950 on the leisure activities of grammar school children. This study found that sport was the favourite out-of-school activity for both boys and girls while, for girls, reading followed a close second. Schofield's (178:169) study was also relevant here. He asked subjects what they had been doing on the evening before the interview and on the previous Saturday night. He found that the most popular activities were:

---

[1] For a complete copy of the final version of the questionnaire, see Appendix D.

Activity	Boys Weekday	Saturday	Girls Weekday	Saturday
TV	*†	*	*	*
Visited friends	*	*	*	*
Drink in pub	*	*	*	*
Study at home	*			*
Sport	*			
Records	*	*	*	*
Cinema	*	*	*	*
Coffee bar	*	*	*	*
Youth club	*			
Friends at home	*		*	
Other club		*		
Dance		*		*
Party		*		*

† = at least 5 per cent of subjects indicated they did this.

Two other studies which included questions on leisure activities were the Government Social Survey's study of cigarette smoking (95) and Veness's study (198) of school leavers. Veness (198:185–7) found that the most popular leisure activities were part-time work, sport, social activities, cinema, radio, reading and gardening. In designing the question on leisure attention was paid to these findings. Consideration was also given to the reputation of the West End for drug-taking (Brain Report (102: paras. 10:12)) and rumours of bowling alleys as being the haunts of drug pushers.

As regards studies about the adolescent's relationship with his parents, Schofield's (178:143) work again proved useful. He found, for example, that sexually experienced teenagers were less likely to refer to their parents with a personal problem than were inexperienced teenagers.

As regards the overall design of this section, there is a considerable debt to the first section of the Government Social Survey's (95) questionnaire on cigarette smoking which covered much of the same ground without the need to disguise its aim.

Though all these studies contributed ideas, the main aim in the final design of the section was to choose questions whose answers would enable the relevant hypotheses to be tested.

Section B

This section consists of a series of attitudinal items measuring hypotheses to do with: relationships with parents, parental control, relationships with peers and ego strength. In the final version there were six sets of items:

1 Items 2, 9, 17, 22, 28 measuring a subject's past relationship with his father.

2 Items 5, 13, 19, 26, 32 measuring subject's present relationship with his mother.

3 Items 6, 11, 20, 24, 29, 33 measuring degree of perceived parental control.

4 Items 4, 8, 10, 15, 23, 31 measuring degree of perceived parental leniency.

5 Items 3, 14, 18, 27, 30, 34 measuring ego strength.

6 Items 1, 7, 12, 16, 21, 25 measuring perceived relationships with peers.

As all human interaction 'is mediated by the feelings, thoughts and perceptions that individuals have about each other' (Secord and Backman 181), it appeared important to measure these when considering the determinants of behaviour. This was because action seemed to be determined by what was perceived by the person to exist rather than what objectively existed. For example, if one finds that a parent decrees that a teenager ought to be in at night by 11 p.m., this information is comparatively meaningless unless one knows whether the child perceives this as being fair or unfair. Only if we have this additional information can we say that a child believes his parents to be lenient or strict with him. As attitudes 'refer to certain regularities on individual's feelings, thoughts and predispositions to act towards some aspect of his environment' (Secord and Backman 181:95) these seemed to be the most appropriate measures to use.

Ideally there should have been a separate attitudinal questionnaire for each set of items but the time available within the schools did not permit this. This resulted in the questionnaire being composed of six different sets of items.

The first two sets concentrate on past relationships with the father and present relationships with the mother because the review of the literature seemed to suggest that these were likely to be the times when the relationships would be most crucial for the subject. The fact that there are two sets of items measuring parental control, one on degree of control and one on degree of leniency, was because the component analysis in the pilot stage indicated that these might be separate factors.

The items on peer group relationships complement some of the questions in section A which elicited the amount of time a subject spent with his peers and whom he took his problems to. Again, however, it is important to know whether for instance being alone a great deal worries the subject or not. If one does not know this, one is likely to work on the premise that a person who spends much of his spare time alone is likely to be more disturbed than someone who answers that they are very peer group orientated. This might not always prove true.

The final set of items is used to measure a personality. Schofield (178:182) used an attitude scale in a similar manner though he factored a total attitudinal questionnaire rather than just having a small number of items. His factor analysis produced two third-order factors for boys and three for girls which he compared to Eysenck's two basic social attitude dimensions of tough-mindedness and radicalism. In this case, where the literature suggested that personality was not as important as other factors in determining the occasional drug use most likely to be found among school children, it was decided to see whether one set of items would do as an indicator. Ideally a more detailed personality questionnaire of proven validity and reliability should have been used, as for example Carey's (37) use of the Cattell's 16PF in his study of compulsive gamblers. However, this takes at least an hour to fill in and interviews with headmasters had indicated that this was all the time likely to be available for the total questionnaire administration.

Section C

This section was designed to see if there was any difference in the value structure of drug-takers and non drug-takers. The section consists of a paired choice questionnaire where subjects have to choose from one of two alternative statements. As the main interest lay in the differences expressed and not in the ranking of these differences it was decided to use this method rather than the longer and more formal paired comparisons procedure.

The items were based first, on the participant observation studies where the way of life observed emphasised a rejection of material values, stressed the present rather than planning for the future, and a paranoid attitude towards the police. A second source for the questionnaire was A. K. Cohen's (48) list of middle-class values.[1] Thirdly, some of the items were adapted from the relevant part of the questionnaire used by Chein *et al.* (45:412–13) where subjects were asked to agree or disagree with a number of statements about life. It was felt that a paired choice design, in contrast to that of Chein *et al.*, enabled one to see if subjects made a consistent rejection of one way of life for another.

Sections D, E and H

These sections consist of perceptual scales measuring perception of self in section D, perception of the ideal self in E, and perception of drug-takers in H. Each scale consists of the same nineteen items on a three-point semantic differential scale. These scales were taken from the Government Social Survey's study of cigarette smoking (95).[2] The only adaptation has been to change the wording to make them suitable for co-educational schools as they were originally designed only for boys.

Section F

This section is a measure of knowledge about drugs and drug terminology. The only available questionnaire in the literature on this topic was one used by Chein *et al.* (45). It was not possible to use it in this case because its items were relevant only to the American situation and because it concentrated solely upon the opiates.

The sources for the items used in this questionnaire were the participant observation studies and the literature. As the literature itself was not always unanimous as to what the effects of a drug were, for example whether amphetamines produced physical dependence or not, it was sometimes difficult to phrase questions so that there was only one correct answer possible. The second difficulty was that drug effects are normally reported in the literature in terms of the general response. However, because the

---

[1] These were discussed in detail in Chapter 5, p. 67.

[2] For a more detailed account of the scales' construction see McKennell and Bynner (153).

effects can vary on each administration, depending on the strength of the dosage, mood and experience of the drug-taker, and so on, it is possible that someone basing his answers on only one drug experience might find that they were not in accord with what was generally reported. Though this in itself would be an interesting finding it was felt that it was also slightly unfair to the occasional taker. To compensate for this it was decided to divide the question-naire into two parts: the first and main part being concerned with factual knowledge, while the second consisted of questions on colloquial drug terminology, a field in which the drug user should have had an advantage over the non-user. The design of this second part was itself complicated by the fact that drugs are referred to by one name in one district and by another in a different area. Therefore only colloquial words about drugs which appeared in many different contexts were used.

A final difficulty in the design of this section was that the drug-taking pattern is continually changing. This meant that if one was going to have questions which could be affected by this change not only was the questionnaire in need of constant revision but also that all subjects would have to be tested, as nearly as possible, at the same time.

Section G

This section was used to measure attitudes to drugs. The Likert method of scaling was used because

the Likert scales tend to perform very well when it comes to a reliable, rough ordering of people with regard to a particular attitude. Apart from their relative ease of construction these scales have . . . other advantages: first they provide more precise information about the respondent's degree of agree-ment or disagreement and respondents usually prefer this to a simple agree/disagree score (Oppenheim 224:141).

The item pool was collected from newspaper cuttings, inter-views with drug-takers and the participant observation studies. Once assembled the scale was constructed with the use of a pilot sample in accordance with the procedure laid down by Edwards (218).

Section I

This is a projective scale involving a number of sentence completion items. Of the eight items only three are of prime interest: items 2, 4 and 5, which are concerned with drug-taking. It was hoped that the first of these, question 2, could be used as an internal check on admission of drug-taking. Question 2 was also concerned with discovering whether the pattern of the first drug-taking experience was related to subsequent drug usage. Question 4 was aimed at obtaining an up to date list of colloquial drug terminology. The previous lists issued (for example by Leech and Jordan 139:113–19) were, because of the rapidly changing drug culture, in need of revision. Finally question 5 was concerned at seeing whether a drug-taker's overall impression of his drug experiences was a determining factor in his continuing use.

The remaining five items were mainly there for padding, to disguise again that the questionnaire was primarily interested in drug-taking. There was a reason though in the choice of items 6 and 7: a social worker in the second participant observation study had noted that many of the members of the club had felt that there was not much future in the world. If this were correct it is possible that some of the members might have argued that if the future is so bleak it does not really matter how damaging the effects of drugs are. It seemed worth seeing if this was an assumption made by those who tried drugs.

Section J

In the second part of the sample an additional page was added to the back of the questionnaires. This asked subjects first, to estimate the numbers of children in the school who smoked, took drugs and drank alcohol; secondly, it asked for their comments on the questionnaire.

The first part was introduced to assist the solution of the problem of how to discover how accurately the questionnaire was measuring the actual drug-taking situation. The other part of this section was introduced during the administration of the questionnaire to the first part of the sample, when those children who finished before the others were asked to write their comments of the questionnaires on the back of the last sheet. As a preliminary glance at these suggested that they might contain useful material in connection with the question of confidentiality, for example, it was decided to include a question on these comments for the second part of the sample to answer.

PILOT STUDY

Aims

The aims of the pilot study were:

1 to ascertain if school children would admit to taking drugs. An educational psychologist, attached to one of the Education Authorities, had written to say: 'I think you would find it exceedingly difficult to identify pupils who are taking drugs, if in fact such cases exist.'

2 to select those hypotheses for testing in the main survey which appeared to differentiate between drug-takers and non-drug-takers.

3 to discover at which age the highest prevalence of drug-taking occurred.

4 to see if there was any significant differences between the sexes in the incidence of drug-taking.

5 to develop precise scales from the pilot questionnaires to be used in the main study.

The sample

The pilot study was carried out in June 1967 in a comprehensive school outside London. Questionnaires were given to seventy out of the 120 pupils who were leaving school that year. Those who had taken the C.S.E. exams had already left. All seventy were tested in one sitting.

Results

The results of the pilot study, in terms of the aims, were:

AIM 1

Ten per cent, or seven of the seventy subjects, admitted having taken drugs of either the cannabis or amphetamine groups. An eighth subject, who said that he took LSD 1–5 times a week was obviously boasting as evidenced by his inadequate knowledge about the drug. This figure of 10 per cent appeared to be most significant at the time because the school was said to be situated in a comparatively low drug rate area and because there had been no reported incidences of drug-taking within the school. However, later in the year a psychiatrist working in the district reported that there was a considerable drug-taking problem in the area involving youths of all ages and all types of drugs. The pilot study did therefore demonstrate that school children were prepared to admit drug-taking behaviour.

AIM 2

The number of hypotheses was reduced from thirty-eight to thirty. This reduction did not change the general areas covered by the survey as it only involved making more precise hypotheses within the categories already decided upon.

AIM 3

The breakdown by age of the subjects in the pilot study was:

Age	Drug-takers	Non-drug-takers
14	—	7
15	5	30
16	1	14
17	1	6
18	—	6

As the proportion of drug-takers in each category approximately followed the overall age group figures for the sample this seemed to indicate that there was no particular age group among school leavers that the main study should concentrate on.

AIM 4

As in most cases of delinquency 'boys constitute the main problem in England . . . at the younger age levels the incidence of convictions of females is only about a tenth that of males' (West 203:15), it might have been expected that the drug-taking problem would be found only among the boys. However, of the seven drug-takers, four were male and three were female. As this is roughly proportionate to the number of males and females in the total sample (42 males: 28 females) it seemed sensible to include both sexes in the main sample.

AIM 5

The following changes were made in the various sections of the questionnaire:

Section A. Changes were made in the design and layout of this section, for example in making sure that all the questions referring to one particular topic were all on the same page. And a section on job choice was deleted and replaced by a single question asking subjects the name of the job they would most like to do. This was done for three reasons. First, because no differences were found between the drug-takers and the non-drug-takers on the series of pilot questions on this topic; secondly, from a time aspect, the questionnaire had to be slightly reduced in length; and thirdly, because many of the job choice alternatives were already included in questions in Section C.

Section B. From a component analysis[1] carried out on the pilot questionnaire, there appeared to be five identifiable factors that the questionnaire was measuring. They were parental control, parental leniency, relation with peers, relation with mother and relation with father. Questions which had the highest loadings on these factors were retained and other questions were added so as to produce a range of questions for each factor. Six further questions were included to measure the personality variable, ego strength.

Section C. This questionnaire was reduced from thirty to seventeen items. The final items were chosen on two criteria. The first was to choose those items which differentiated best between drug-takers and non-drug-takers. The second criterion was to choose items which had as close to a 50/50 distribution on the two parts for the total sample.

Sections D. E. and H. In the pilot stage only two scales, a self perception and a perception of drug-takers, similar in design but not identical to those in the final stage, were used. A component analysis was carried out on the two scales and the results, as might have been expected, showed that subjects perceived themselves in a more favourable manner than the way in which they perceived drug-takers.

It was decided in the final survey to use the same scales as those used by the Government Social Survey (95) in their study

---

[1] This will be discussed in more detail in Chapter 8.

of cigarette smoking because in addition to providing the same type of information as the pilot scales did, they also offered a possibility of a comparison being made with the perception of cigarette smokers.

Section F. This questionnaire was given to a group of institutionalised addicts as an additional pilot. This was to try to eliminate questions where either a true or false answer would have been equally correct and to standardise the drug terminology.

Only slight changes were made in the final version as the questionnaire seemed to be working well. The changes that were made were: first, in the wording of some questions; secondly, the substitution of three questions where there was some doubt as to the right answer; and thirdly, the substitution of some questions, particularly in the second part, to make sure there was a balance of questions about each of the different types of drugs.

A factor analysis was carried out on the pilot questionnaire to see if the different drug groups formed distinct factors. However, the factors that did emerge were not easily identifiable and it seemed that knowledge about drugs was general and not specific to any one drug.

Section G. The choice of items in this attitudinal scale was done by following Edwards's procedure for the design of Likert scales (218). By this process the scale was reduced from forty to seventeen items.

Section I. In the pilot study only two of the drug questions that were in the final draft were included (questions 2 and 4 in the final version). As the results of both of these looked interesting it was decided to include a third drugs question in the final version (i.e. question 5). The results of the two pilot questions on drugs were:

Question 2. The first time I took drugs (answers given are those of the seven drug-takers).

    (*a*) I felt good but a little sick. I decided to do it again (cannabis).

    (*b*) I felt all right (cannabis).

    (*c*) was when I was with a lot of boys (pep pills).

    (*d*) was round a girl's house one morning. It was the best feeling I ever had (cannabis).

(*e*) was a disappointing occurrence—highly overrated (pep pills).

(*f*) I was sick (pep pills).

(*g*) I felt all right (cannabis).

On the question about drug names the sixteen subjects who had the most favourable attitudes to drugs on Section G gave an average of 4·2 names while the subjects with the least favourable attitudes gave an average of only two names per person. Besides the possibility of using this question as another means of differentiating drug-takers and non-drug-takers, many colloquial terms were reported.[1]

As regards the other questions, two were discarded because their answers were so random as to be uncategorisable in any manner and they were replaced by questions 6 and 7 in the final version which were concerned with the subjects' perception of the future of the world.

---

[1] See Chapter 8 for a complete list.

7 Selection of schools and the procedure of questionnaire administration

SIZE OF THE SAMPLE

Working from the fact that 10 per cent of the pilot sample admitted taking drugs, it was calculated that a sample of about 1000 children should result in a large enough number of drug-takers to be able to make significant comparisons between them and a control group. At the time the decision was made the psychiatrist's report on the true drug incidence figures in the pilot area was not yet available, but it was felt that as the survey was attempting to select schools with a suspected drug problem, the 10 per cent response estimate was a conservative figure.

SELECTION OF SCHOOLS

Letters were sent to eleven education authorities.[1] Nine of these were adjacent to London and two were outside London. The authorities were chosen partly on the basis of whether there had been any press publicity about drug-taking in that area and partly to give some degree of geographical representation.

Replies were received from ten of the authorities. Of the ten, four had no objection to the experimenter writing to the headmasters in their district and two went as far as enclosing a list of the schools within their borough. Of the other six, one said that there was 'soon' to be a meeting of headmasters within the borough

---

[1] See Appendix E1.

to discuss the problem of drug-taking and the project would be put to them then. At this meeting, which did not take place for another two months, the headmasters decided not to cooperate. Of the remaining five authorities, one said that they were already making their own enquiries about the problem and that anyway they were overresearched. Another said that they had 'decided the best way to treat this problem at the moment is to play it cool and not to encourage general and continued discussion on drug taking'. Another said that they did not normally agree to this type of survey, and a fourth said that they were too heavily involved in reorganisation and it would not therefore be convenient for the headmasters. The fifth did not believe that the study was feasible.

The next step was to choose the schools in each of the four boroughs which were most likely to have a problem and to discover in general terms the drug-taking pattern in each of the four areas.

There were a number of different approaches possible. It was decided to approach one agency only. The one chosen in three of the boroughs was the probation service. This was first, because they would be likely to know of most of the cases which appeared before the local courts; secondly, because many of the probation offices had one member who concentrated on drug offences; thirdly (and consequently) the probation service appeared to have a good idea of the extent of the local drug problem. In the fourth borough the probation service recommended that the deputy medical officer of health be approached as he was interested in the problem. As he seemed to have a good knowledge of the local situation his recommendations were followed.

A letter asking for an appointment, was written to the probation offices in each of the four boroughs.[1] In some boroughs more than one office was involved. All the probation offices written to agreed to a meeting.

At the meeting the probation officers were asked:

1 whether there was any drug-taking in the area;
2 if not, whether they knew of young people going outside the area to places like Soho where they might take drugs;
3 if so, whether they knew of places in the area where drugs were pushed;

---

[1] See Appendix E.

4 whether they knew of any school children frequenting these places;

5 if they knew of any specific schools which had a drug problem, and if yes, whether this was based on fact or rumour;

6 to choose three schools in the area which they felt to have the biggest drug problem or which were most likely to have a drug problem;

7 if this proved impossible, to choose the schools with the highest delinquency rate. This was because the literature suggested that drug-taking might be just one form of delinquency.

From this interview it was possible to obtain some idea of the prevalence of drug-taking in each area. Relative to each other, one area could be said to have had a high incidence of drug-taking, two a medium and one a low incidence.

The general drug-taking situation in each area

THE HIGH AREA

There appeared to be little cannabis in the district and what there was seemed to be confined to the immigrant population. There was a large group of 17/18-year-olds who took pep pills. Members of this group worked only part-time and many of the females did a bit of prostitution on the side. The probation officer interviewed said that many of this group seemed to be habitual users of pills and some of the group were also occasional heroin users. As regards heroin the probation officer said that out of a case load of twenty-seven he had eight heroin addicts. In a typical month there were ten drug cases passing through the courts. In the week prior to the interview there had been four cases. The probation officer knew of four places in the district where drugs were available but commented that the local police were comparatively uninterested in the problem. The probation officer said that whereas some of the brighter children went to Soho to obtain and take their drugs, the dimmer, labouring types took theirs locally. He estimated that the total number of drug-takers in the district would be in the hundreds.

MEDIUM AREA

As all the headmasters in one of the medium areas turned the survey down, this description is restricted to the other medium area.

Cannabis again was restricted to the immigrant population but pep pills were freely available. There was no heroin problem. This was because when they left school many of the youngsters moved out of the district because there were few opportunities for them in the area. Pep pills were known to circulate freely at teenage parties and there were also three known places within the area where drugs could be bought, though a recent police raid at one had failed to find any evidence of this. The reason given for the easy availability of pills in the area was that most were stolen from a nearby chemical factory. Another reason was that pills were believed to be less dangerous than hashish which was looked on as a hard drug. Few people from the area went to Soho. In conclusion the probation officer said that the problem tended to be restricted to pills because the people who were likely to take the other drugs were the ones who would have most probably moved out of the area. The main deviancy problem in the district as far as they were concerned was promiscuity.

LOW AREA

There appeared to be no drug-taking in this area. At a recent conference of headmasters in the district no one had reported any drug-taking episodes in their school. The local probation officer was unable to name any 'den of vice' in the district, while the police had raided the local 'Palais' frequently with no results. If there was any drug-taking it would have been when and if the locals went up to the West End for the night or weekend.

School chosen

As the basic aim of the sampling procedure was to maximise the number of drug-takers, letters were written to four headmasters in the high drug area, to three in each of the medium drug areas and to two in the low drug area.

HIGH DRUG AREA

In this area there were sixteen schools, all of which were comprehensive. Five were denominational. Letters were written to four of the remaining eleven schools. One was chosen because it was known that about a year before boys from this school had been invited to LSD parties and it was also known that some boys there took pills. Two of the other schools were chosen because they had a high delinquency rate and the fourth was included because it was situated in a high delinquency area. Of the four schools approached, three agreed to cooperate. The fourth declined because it did not wish to take part in anything which might disturb the running of the school.

The first school had been formed from the amalgamation of two secondary modern schools. It had a total of 1568 male and female pupils of whom approximately 130 were leaving school that year. About 36 per cent of the pupils were immigrants. The headmaster, in describing the catchment area, said that it was a working-class industrial district and that many of the fathers were employed as transport workers.

The second school was formed from the joining of a grammar school and a secondary modern school. It had 840 male pupils of whom 126 were school leavers. According to the headmaster the grammar school boys had primarily middle-class origins while the ex-secondary modern school boys came from working-class homes.

The third school was also formed by a coalition of a grammar and a secondary modern school. There were a total of 1222 male and female pupils in the school of whom 510 were in school leaving forms. The headmaster said that it was administratively impossible to separate the school leavers from the remainder of the pupils in these forms so, as the school was in a high drug area and as the aim was to maximise the number of drug-takers in the sample, it was decided to include all the school leaving forms. The headmaster said that the ex-grammar school pupils came mainly from a lower-middle-class background and their fathers were often employed or employers in the clerical and retail trades. The ex-secondary modern school children came mainly from upper-working-class areas and many of their fathers were transport workers. Fifteen per cent of the school population consisted of immigrant children. The headmaster also mentioned that he had had a suspicion that about two years previously some pupils had tried drugs as a temporary experiment.

MEDIUM DRUG AREA (1)

All three headmasters approached declined to participate in the survey. Two gave no reason while the third headmaster said that drugs had already been discussed in his school and any further information upon it would only receive a bored reaction.

MEDIUM DRUG AREA (2)

In this area there were twenty-seven secondary schools, fifteen of which were mixed, six were boys only and six were girls only. Letters were sent to three headmasters. In this area no school had a known drug problem and the probation officers said that the delinquency problem was dispersed through all the schools. Finally one was chosen because it had a reputation for being a fairly rough school, another because it catered for council house children, and the third simply because it was in a different geographical part of the area. Two of the headmasters agreed to cooperate and one declined for no stated reason.

The first school was a mixed secondary modern. It had 350 pupils of whom 105 were school leavers. The catchment area was working class and 18 per cent of the pupils were immigrants.

The second school was also a mixed secondary modern. It had 401 pupils of whom 85 were said to be school leavers. Most pupils came from a local council house estate.

LOW AREA

There were seventeen secondary schools in this borough. Four were mixed, six had only boys and seven had only girls. Letters were sent to two headmasters. One of these was chosen because his school was said to contain a complete cross-section of the population in the district and the second because of a reported rumour in the area about someone from that school taking drugs. Only one of the two headmasters agreed to cooperate so a letter was sent to a third headmaster but he eventually also declined because he feared that the questionnaire might arouse too much interest in the topic.

The one school in this area was a boys' secondary modern school. It had 450 pupils of whom 70 were school leavers. The catchment area was lower middle class and working class and about half the pupils came from council homes.

Summary

This left six schools in the first part of the sample. These, arranged in the order in which the survey was carried out, were:

Type	Area	No. of estimated school leavers
1 Comprehensive	High drug	130
2 Comprehensive	High drug	510
3 Secondary modern	Low drug	70
4 Secondary modern	Medium drug	85
5 Secondary modern	Medium drug	105
6 Comprehensive	High drug	126
	Total	1026

Administrative arrangements with the school

Once a headmaster had agreed to take part in the survey or had requested more information, an interview was arranged. At this meeting the headmaster, once he had confirmed his willingness to cooperate, was asked if it were possible:

1 for all the subjects to be assembled together for the one hour that the questionnaire took to complete;
2 for there to be no teachers present during the administration of the survey;
3 for him, when discussing it with other members of staff or with pupils, to refer to it as a survey about the general problems of youth without referring specifically to drugs.

All the headmasters were good enough to agree on these points though one pointed out that the children would probably have to be in two rooms.

The headmasters were then asked if they wished the parents to be notified beforehand but they all felt this was unnecessary and that they would be able to deal with any complaints that might arise. If the headmaster requested it, he was given a copy of the questionnaire. Finally a date was fixed for the survey to be carried out.

ADMINISTRATION OF THE QUESTIONNAIRES TO THE FIRST PART OF THE SAMPLE

The surveys at all six schools were carried out within the week of 15–22 February 1968. In each case the experimenter, assisted by two graduate social psychologists, conducted the survey.

Even though the conditions varied from school to school, the general procedure was the same. The headmaster would introduce the research team, saying that they were there to find out what the pupils thoughts were about things in general and stressing the survey's confidentiality; usually they pointed out that it was not compulsory to complete it. The headmaster then left and the standard introduction[1] was read out to all the subjects. The time

---

[1] See Appendix E4.

taken to complete the questionnaire varied from thirty-five minutes for the brightest sixth-formers to an hour for the less intelligent fourth-formers.

Final total

Owing to last minute administrative changes in two of the schools and to absenteeism in the others, the total number of pupils who completed questionnaires was 794 instead of the estimated 1026. As the percentage who admitted to taking drugs was also below that expected (5·2 per cent instead of 10 per cent) it was decided to draw a second sample of approximately 450 subjects.

THE SECOND SAMPLE

The health department of a borough in London completed an interview survey of headmasters in its district and reported its results just after the administration of the questionnaires to the first part of the sample. The health department found that nine out of the fifteen headmasters seen said that they had some sort of drug problem within their school. In its conclusion the report recommended that a fuller study should be carried out to determine the true extent of the drug-taking problem among the schoolchildren in its borough. When the experimenter approached the health committee they agreed to cooperate, because they felt that this survey would go a long way towards meeting their report's recommendation. The health department made the provision that an attempt should be made to draw as representative a sample as possible of the school children within its borough. This was complicated by the fact that the experimenter only required 450 subjects, i.e. about six schools.

The area

From the health department's survey, which also looked at the prevalence of drug-taking in the district, it appeared that this area, in relation to those already sampled, was classifiable as a very high drug area. This was based on the fact that there were known to be many heroin addicts in the area, pep pills were freely available and hashish was widely used. Newspaper reports of drug arrests frequently named places within this borough.

SCHOOLS CHOSEN

It was decided to try to make the sample representative of both
type of school and of geographical area. The area could then be
divided as follows:

GEOGRAPHICAL AREA 1

3 boys' secondary modern schools
1 mixed secondary modern school
2 boys' grammar schools.

GEOGRAPHICAL AREA 2

2 mixed secondary modern schools
1 girls' secondary modern school
1 boys' grammar school
1 girls' grammar school
1 boys' secondary technical school.

GEOGRAPHICAL AREA 3

3 mixed secondary modern schools
1 girls' grammar school
1 girls' comprehensive school.

Ideally, therefore, if one wanted to choose schools representative
of both type and area, two schools would be required from each
district, representative of the type of school in the area and totally
in the proportion of four secondary modern schools to two grammar schools, with three mixed to one boys' secondary modern
schools.

However, it was important to include the comprehensive school
in place of one of the mixed secondary modern schools as it was
the biggest school in the borough. This therefore left the following:

Area 1 1 boys' secondary modern school
1 boys' grammar school.
Area 2 1 mixed secondary modern school
1 girls' grammar school.
Area 3 1 mixed secondary modern school
1 girls' comprehensive.

The next ideal step would have been to select the particular schools within each category on a random basis. However, the original report had indicated that only twelve of the seventeen headmasters would be likely to cooperate. This conveniently left one appropriate school for each category.

The department of health was also asked to rate the schools in the area in terms of the likelihood of their having a serious drug problem. This was in line with the method used to select the schools in the first stage of the sample. It turned out that all of the six schools chosen on a representative basis were among the first seven schools selected on a drug potential basis.

Once the schools had been agreed on, permission was sought from the local education authority. The authority eventually agreed to let the survey take place provided first, that they made the initial approach to the headmaster, and secondly, that if headmasters required it, parents should be given the opportunity of withholding their permission for their child to take part. The first condition had the disadvantage that one was unable to fully utilise the relationship already built up between the health department and the headmasters.

Of the six schools selected, three declined to participate when contacted by the local education authority and three agreed to meet the experimenter. A further three schools were then contacted by the authority, two of which were also on the health department's list of schools with a suspected drug problem. Of these three schools, one turned the project down and two agreed to meet the experimenter.

Of the five schools the experimenter visited, three agreed to cooperate. Of the two that declined one felt that the questionnaire administration might affect the equilibrium of the school while the other felt that a relationship was being established with the pupils on the problem of drug-taking and that the questionnaire might prove detrimental to that *rapport*.

This left three schools. The first was a girls' grammar school with about 500 pupils. It was decided to include the whole of the upper sixth, who were all leavers and the whole of the fifth form, including both the leavers and non-leavers as it was too difficult administratively to separate them. The head estimated that this would involve about 106 pupils. The head of the school had reported in the health department's survey that there was a small drug problem in the school. The experimenter heard rumours from other sources that girls from this school were involved in drug parties.

The second school was a boys' grammar school with about 550

pupils. It also had a reported drug problem. Owing to the close-ness of the 'O' and 'A' level exams, it was agreed that only the fourth form (N=90–100) would take part. The headmaster said that if there was a problem in the school it was likely that one or two of the fourth formers would be responsible.

The third school was a boys' comprehensive (though until recently it was called a secondary modern school) with about 720 pupils. In this school, which had no reported problem, the leavers from the sixth, fifth and fourth forms took part. Their numbers were estimated to be about 150.

It can therefore be seen that the final sample was by no means representative of the schools in the district, for example instead of there being twice as many secondary modern/comprehensive schools compared to grammar schools, the proportion was in fact reversed.

Actual Administration

The general procedure was the same as in the first part of the sample. Again all the schools were surveyed within the space of one week, 28–31 May 1968.

Final total

The original estimate had been that 351 pupils would fill in questionnaires. Owing to absenteeism only 299 questionnaires were completed. This gave a final total sample of 1093 which was close to the required number of 1000 subjects.

PART THREE

Results, Discussion and Recommendations

8 Results

THE SAMPLE

Questionnaires were given to 1093 subjects. Three of the questionnaires were discarded because the subjects did not understand enough English to complete them competently. For the purpose of description the sample can be divided into the four areas of low, medium, high and very high drug use. The complete breakdown sample, school by school, is given in Appendix A.

The number and sex distribution of subjects

Area	No. of schools	Code no. of schools	Total no. of pupils	Male pupils	Female pupils
Low	1	3	67	35	32
Medium	2	4:5	144	75	69
High	3	1:2:6	583	335	248
Very high	3	7:8:9	299	209	90
Total	9		1093	654	439

In keeping with the original intention, the sample was biased in favour of overrepresentation from the high drug areas. In fact 80·6 per cent of the sample came from these two areas. As it can also be seen, there were more male than female pupils, 59·5 per cent to 41·5 per cent, especially in the very high area.

SAMPLE BY AGE (*figures in percentages*)

Area	14	15	16	17	18	19
Low	25	45	30			
Medium	32	50	16	1	1	
High	25	41	19	10	3	2
Very high	5	43	36	8	7	1
Total	20	44	24	8	4	1

As can be seen from the table, the very high area has a higher proportion of 16 + -year-olds to 14-year-olds, while the reverse is true for the medium area. These differences are significant at the 5 per cent level as tested by Zubin's Nomographs. As 87·4 per cent of the sample are aged 16 years or under it can be seen that the sample has a high proportion of the lower leaving forms compared to the sixth form.

SAMPLE BY SOCIAL CLASS[1] (*percentages*)

Area	Classes 1/2	Classes 3/4	Class 5a	Class 5b	Classes 6/7	No answer
Low	5	24	9	43	16	3
Medium	—	11	8	44	22	15
High	10	22	8	37	11	12
Very high	21	24	10	33	3	9
Total	12	21	8	37	11	11

As the table shows by far the largest part of the sample came from class 5b (skilled manual) and classes 3/4 (inspectional, supervisory and other non-manual, higher and lower grades). They accounted for 58 per cent of the subjects. It is interesting that there is comparatively little difference between the four groups in the pattern of social class, though the very high area has a higher proportion of subjects in classes 1/2 and a lower proportion in classes 6/7 in comparison to the other three areas. The fact that 11 per cent of subjects did not answer this question might well be an indication that this is not a particularly meaningful question to ask many school children.

Trouble with the police (*percentages*)

Area	Yes	No
Low	16	84
Medium	19	81
High	19	81
Very high	18	82
Total	19	81

[1] Social class was determined on the basis of the Hall-Jones Scale. This scale is given in Dr Oppenheim's *Questionnaire Design and Attitude Measurement*, Heinemann Educational Books, 1966.

The figures here are remarkable for their consistency in distribution from area to area with nearly 1 in 5 of the children sampled admitting that they have been in trouble with the police.

School leaver

An attempt was originally made to obtain wherever possible children who were going to leave school by the end of the year. As has already been seen this proved to be administratively very difficult. In fact only 39·2 per cent of the subjects turned out to be school leavers, 59·9 per cent were staying on and 0·9 per cent did not know. Therefore, though the sample is biased in favour of the areas with the highest incidence of drug-taking; on the variables of age, social class, sex and trouble with the police there is a great deal of similarity between the low, medium and high areas, with the very high area differing from the others on its social class and age distribution. The medium area also differs from the others in terms of the age distribution.

THE DRUG-TAKERS

Checks

The first criterion, by which it was determined whether subjects took drugs or not, were their answers to questions 26 and 27 in Questionnaire A. To be included as a drug-taker a subject had to indicate on both of the questions that he took drugs. On the basis of these questions sixty-four subjects were provisionally classified as drug-takers. Each of these subjects' answers was then submitted to consistency checks within the questionnaire. The first of these was to see if their answers to questions 2 and 5 in Questionnaire I made sense in light of their answer to question 27 (Questionnaire A). A further check was made on subjects who said that they took drugs on a regular basis. It was assumed that if subjects took drugs regularly they would also know other people who took drugs and a check was therefore made with their answer to question 10, Questionnaire A. A final check was made on regular drug users upon whom there was still some doubt as to whether they were drug-takers. In this case it was assumed that subjects who took drugs frequently would have some knowledge about the effects of these drugs. A check was therefore made on their answers to the appropriate questions in Questionnaire F.

On the basis of these checks, five questionnaires were discarded.

Three of these were the questionnaires discarded because of the subjects' lack of English. In the other two cases the subjects' answers to questions 2 and 5 in Questionnaire I did not tally with their stated drug-taking behaviour. This left fifty-nine subjects who were classified as drug-takers, i.e. 5·39 per cent of the sample.

Accuracy of the figure

It would have been possible to have treated questions 2 and 5 in Questionnaire I as a type of projective test to determine whether children took drugs or not, and used these answers as the sole criteria. What is interesting, or perhaps methodologically disturbing, is that 153 'non-drug-takers' gave the type of answers to these questions that would have been expected from someone who had taken drugs. The reason for this, from the comments of two of the subjects who were questioned about it, is that the subjects treated these questions as 'fantasy' tests to which they had to make up sensible answers. It is possible though that there might have been subjects who took drugs, did not admit so in Questionnaire A, but did answer Questionnaire I in the light of their drug-taking experience. It is, however, impossible to check this.

This is one reason for thinking that, if anything, the figure of 5·39 per cent is an underestimation of the number of drug-takers in the sample. A second reason is that in every school there were a number of children absent. For example, in the second part of the sample 14·8 per cent fewer children completed questionnaires than the number originally given by the headmasters who would do so. Some of those absent would obviously have been sick, but others would have been truants. Research, for example that of Hersov (104), has shown that truancy can be either a symptom of neurotic behaviour or of delinquency. As will be shown later a high percentage of the drug-takers in this sample were delinquents. It is possible therefore that a number of those children who were absent might have been drug-takers. This argument is supported by the fact that Hawks et al. (100) in their study of regular methylamphetamine users found that 'consistent truancy was relatively common in secondary schools being reported in 43 per cent of cases. A further 8 per cent were occasionally truant.' It should also be pointed out that in most cases it would only be truants who would be able to take drugs on a daily basis while still at school. A third reason is that in some schools not all the school leaving forms were included and as will be shown later drug-takers are more likely than others to be school leavers. For these reasons it would appear that the 5·39 per cent figure is a conservative estimate and that the truer or more accurate figure might be between 7 per cent and 10 per cent.

What can be deduced from these figures about the school population as a whole? It must first be pointed out that as this survey only included school leaving forms, the figure of 7–10 per cent is probably a slight underestimation of the total drug-taking behaviour in these schools. This is because, as will be shown later, drug-taking does occur among children as young as 13 and 14. Therefore, considering all children in these schools, a figure of 10 per cent who have tried drugs is perhaps the most realistic. This would be in keeping with Binnie's findings (23). A second point is that as the sample in this survey is not representative in any way of the school population as a whole one cannot directly generalise from its findings. It is, however, possible to make some inferences.

First, drug-taking appears to bear some relation to the general level of drug-taking in a district. The districts in this survey, being in and around London, included some of the areas where one would expect to find as high a level of drug-taking as in any area in England. It can therefore be suggested that the figure of 10 per cent might well be a high estimate of the numbers who take drugs in the big cities. It is probably a high estimate because it must be remembered that the schools in this sample were chosen on the basis of their likelihood of having drug-takers and that the average number of drug-takers for all the schools in any one area would probably therefore be less than the estimated 10 per cent. In any case it is likely that there would be a considerable range between different areas within any city.

However, it must not be assumed that the figure of 10 per cent means that this is the number of subjects who take drugs on a regular basis (for a definition of 'regular' as used here, see below). Of the fifty-nine subjects in this sample 75 per cent were occasional or once only users. If this proportion were the same for the school population at large this would mean that in the big cities 2·5 per cent or less of the school population would be taking drugs regularly. Whatever the figures for drug-taking in the big cities, it is likely that in rural areas and in smaller cities the figures are much lower.

Regular *v.* occasional users

The drug-takers were divided into those who were regular and those who were occasional users.

Occasional users were defined as those who had taken a drug or drugs only once, *or* had taken a drug or drugs less than five times, *or* had now stopped taking this drug or drugs.

Regular users were defined as those who sometimes take this drug or drugs at weekends or parties, *or* take this drug or drugs at least 1–5 times a week.

Of the fifty-nine drug-takers, forty-four or 75 per cent were occasional users and fifteen or 25 per cent were regular users. This means that only 1·4 per cent of the total sample were regular drug users.

TYPE OF DRUG USED[1]

One-drug users	Two-drug users	Three-drug users	Four-drug users
Hashish 12	Pep pills and hashish 8	Pep pills, LSD and hashish 5	Pep pills, hashish, heroin and LSD 1
Pep pills 21			
	Pep pills and LSD 3	Pep pills, hashish and heroin 2	
LSD 1			
Other 1	Hashish and LSD 2	Pep pills, hashish and other 1	
	Hashish and heroin 2		
N = 35	15	8	1

As the table shows 35 of the drug users had tried only one drug. 15 had taken two, 8 had taken three types of drugs and one had taken four. What perhaps is worrying is that five of the subjects said that they had tried heroin. It is slightly more reassuring that three of them had said they had now stopped taking this drug, one said that she had only taken it once and one said that he took it sometimes at weekends or parties.

Another disquieting feature was that twelve of the subjects said that they had used LSD. However of these, as in the case of

---

[1] A complete list for each individual is given in Appendix A.

heroin, only one subject said that he took the drug as frequently as 'sometimes at weekends or parties'. Of the other eleven, six had only taken it once and five had taken it less than five times. A much less alarming feature was that seventeen of the subjects had taken a drug on only one occasion and then stopped taking. This finding, together with the high proportion of occasional to regular users is indicative of a general picture of experimentation rather than one of an onset of a drug epidemic.

SEX DISTRIBUTION OF DRUG-TAKERS (*percentages*)

	Male	Female	N	
Drug-takers	62·8	37·2	59	not significant[1]
Non-drug-takers	59·8	41·2	1031	at 5 per cent level

The proportion of male to female drug-takers in this sample is similar to that for the rest of the sample. This figure is interesting in so far as previous studies have tended to suggest that a disproportionate number of males are found among drug-takers.

DRUG-TAKERS BY AREA

Area	No. of drug-takers	As percentage of pupils tested in that area	Range
Low	2	3	—
Medium	3	2·1	0–3
High	29	4·9	3·7–14·6
Very high	25	8·4	7·7–10·0

The table shows that, excluding the low area in which there was only one school, there is a relationship between the percentage of pupils taking drugs in an area and the general level of drug-taking in that area. Even though the only significant difference between areas is between the medium and the very high area ($X^2 = 5·5$, significant at 2 per cent level) these figures do suggest that this relationship would be worth following up in a future study.

---

[1] Significance levels in this and the following tables are as tested by Zubin's Nomographs.

DRUG-TAKERS BY AGE (*percentages*)

	14	15	16	17	18	19	N
Drug-takers	16·9	32·2	32·2	15·2	3·4	—	59
Non-drug-takers	20·4	43·9	23·2	7·4	3·7	1·3	1031

If the age groups are combined into 15 and under, and 16 and over, the results then are that while 51 per cent of the drug-takers are aged 16 or over only 36 per cent of the non-drug-takers are this old. This difference is significant at the 5 per cent level. The implication of this finding is that drug-takers are more likely to be found among the older school children. This finding clashes with hypothesis 16. This said that the younger a person leaves school, the more likely he is to take drugs. One would therefore have expected that children in the lower school leaving forms would be more likely to take drugs than children in the older forms. In fact drug-takers tended to be found in the older age groups.

DRUG-TAKERS BY SOCIAL CLASS (*percentages*)

	1/2	3/4	5a	5b	6/7	N.A.	N
Drug-takers	16·9	35·6	10·2	23·7	5·1	9	59
Non-drug-takers	11·2	20·6	8·3	37·1	11·1	11	1031

If the social classes are combined into 5a and above (white collar) and 5b and below (blue collar) then while 62·7 per cent of the drug-takers come from white collar families, only 40·1 per cent of the non-drug-takers do. This difference is significant at the 1 per cent level. The result is in direct contradiction to what was originally hypothesised. Hypothesis 1 said that the lower the social class the more likely was a school child to take drugs. The result suggests that drug takers at school are more likely to be found among the higher social classes.

DRUG-TAKERS AS SCHOOL LEAVERS (*percentages*)

	Yes, will leave	No	Don't know
Drug-takers	50·8	45·5	3·4
Non-drug-takers	38·6	60·6	0·8

Compared with the rest of the sample significantly more drug-takers were either planning to leave school by the end of the year or were unsure about their plans. This difference was significant at the 5 per cent level. This finding supports hypothesis 20 which said that children who were about to leave school were more likely to take drugs than were children who had one or more years to go.

Therefore, somewhat against expectations, the drug-takers were representative of the sample as a whole in the ratio of males to females. Against what was hypothesised the drug-takers tended to be older than the rest of the sample and to come from white collar rather than blue collar backgrounds. In line with what was hypothesised drug-takers were more likely to be school leavers than the rest of the sample. Finally it proved impossible to test a second hypothesis on social class, hypothesis 2, which stated that the lower school children perceive their social class to be the more likely they were to take drugs. This was because over 10 per cent of the subjects did not answer this question.

THE CONTROLS

For every drug-taker a control was selected. They were matched on the following variables: (a) same school, (b) same sex, (c) same age, (d) whether a school leaver, and (e) social class. If after matching on these variables there were still a number of non-drug-takers who could have been matched with a particular drug-taker the final selection was made on the basis of the subject's perception of his social class.

The majority of the remainder of the analysis consists of a comparison between the fifty-nine drug-takers and their fifty-nine controls.

STATISTICS USED

In analysing Questionnaire A, two statistical tests have been used. The first of these is the nomographs for the testing of statistical significance of differences between percentages. The test was originally published by Zubin and has been more recently recalculated by Oppenheim (224). As nomographs are somewhat lacking in precision for the more important differences, the chi-square test has been used.

In the other questionnaires, particularly C, the chi-squared and

Zubin's nomographs are used when frequencies are being compared. In much of the analysis of questionnaires B, C and F the test used to measure the significance of differences between the scores of the drug-takers and the controls is the Wilcoxon Matched-Pairs Signed-Ranks Test.

Friedman's Two-Way Analysis of Variance was used to test differences between the two groups on the three concepts measured in Questionnaires D, E and H. Finally the Mann-Whitney U Test was used to measure differences between regular and occasional drug-takers and between male and female drug-takers.

A component analysis was carried out on Questionnaires D, E and H. The method used was identical to that used by Schofield in his study. The actual method used was developed by Hendrikson and White (220), i.e. the matrix was analysed by the principal component method, the first order factors were rotated to oblique simple structure using the Promax method developed by Hendrikson and White and the loadings of the factors on each statement were calculated. All factors with a latent root >1 were extracted.

DRUG-TAKERS COMPARED TO CONTROLS

Family and home conditions

PARENTAL SEPARATION

Subjects were asked whether their mother and father lived in the same house as they did. In both groups, in 94 per cent of the cases the mother did while for 81 per cent of the drug-takers and 89 per cent of the controls the father also lived in the same house. There was therefore no significant difference between the two groups in terms of parental separation.

SIZE OF THE FAMILY

There was similarly no difference in the size of the family of the two groups. Forty per cent of the drug-takers had one or less brothers or sisters while the comparable figure for the controls was 48 per cent.

PRIVACY

The specific hypothesis tested here, no. 7, was that the less privacy school children have at home the more likely they are to take drugs. This was tested by asking the subjects whether they had a room of their own to sleep in and in which to do their homework. The figures show that there was no significant difference between the two groups: 61 per cent of the drug-takers and 66 per cent of the controls slept in a room on their own while 69 per cent of the drug-takers and 61 per cent of the controls had a room of their own in which to do their homework. The hypothesis was therefore rejected.

CONFIDANT

The specific hypothesis tested, no. 29, was that the more school children use peers rather than adults as confidants the more likely they are to take drugs. The figures show that 46 per cent of the drug-takers and 42 per cent of the controls, when asked who they usually talked over a personal problem with, said: 'a close friend of my own age'. There was no significant difference between the two groups. A further analysis of the question showed, however, that whereas 36 per cent of the controls usually referred to one of their two parents, only 13 per cent of the drug-takers did so (difference significant at 5 per cent level). The hypothesis is therefore partly supported, i.e. drug-takers are less likely than controls to refer to their parents but are not necessarily more likely to refer to their peers. The implication of this finding is that drug-takers are not perhaps as close to their parents as the controls still are.

ATTITUDES TO THE FAMILY

Four specific hypotheses were tested here: no. 3, that the less close school children perceive themselves to have been to their father from childhood onwards the more likely they are to take drugs; no. 4, that the closer a male school child feels to his mother and the more distant a female school child feels to her mother, the more likely he is to take drugs; no. 5, that the greater the degree of parental control the less likely school children are to take drugs; and no. 6, that the greater the degree of parental leniency the more likely school children are to take drugs.

In scales one and three there was no significant difference between the two groups ($p=0.0505$ and 0.0668 respectively) and the null hypotheses that there were no significant differences between the two groups cannot therefore be rejected.

On the second scale there was a significant difference in the predicted direction between the female drug-takers and their controls, i.e. the drug-takers felt less close to their mother than the controls did (significant at 1 per cent level). When comparing the males, a significant difference was again found but this time in the reverse direction from that predicted, i.e. the male drug-takers, as did the females, felt less close to their mother than did the controls ($p=0.022$, significant at 5 per cent level). The null hypothesis that there was no difference between the control and the drug-taker groups is rejected and one can accept that both male and female drug-takers feel less close to their mother than do controls.

On the fourth scale there was a significant difference between the two groups ($p=0.001$, significant at 1 per cent level), the drug-takers feeling that their parents were more lenient than the controls felt that their parents were. The fourth hypothesis was therefore accepted.

The drug-takers therefore when compared to the controls felt further away from their mother, though not their father and felt also that their parents were more lenient with them. This partly ties in with the previous finding that the drug-takers are less likely than the controls to refer to their parents when they have a problem.

Performance in school

The specific hypothesis tested, no. 19, was that the worse school children feel they have done at school the more likely they are to take drugs.

DRUG-TAKERS' PERFORMANCE AT SCHOOL

	In the top ten	Just above the middle Below the middle
Drug-takers	20	38 $\chi^2=3.84$ (significant at 5% level)
Controls	31	26

As the table shows, the drug-takers said they did significantly worse at school than the controls said they did. The null hypothesis that there was no significant difference between the two groups is therefore rejected.

Delinquency

TROUBLE WITH THE POLICE

The specific hypothesis tested, no. 14, stated that if school children have been in trouble with the police then they are more likely to take drugs. When subjects were asked whether they had been in trouble with the police it was found that while 57 per cent of the drug-takers had been in trouble with the police only 12 per cent of the controls had (difference significant at 1 per cent level). Though the precise nature of the trouble is not known, for nine of the drug-takers it was sufficiently severe for them to have been put on probation. The hypothesis was therefore supported. The size of the delinquency problem among these drug-takers is perhaps best understood when one realises that 57 per cent of the drug-takers had been in trouble with the police compared with only 16·3 per cent of the 1031 other subjects.

NUMBER OF DELINQUENT FRIENDS

The hypothesis tested here (no. 15) states that the more delinquent friends school children have the more likely they are to take drugs. In the questionnaires subjects were asked how many of their friends had been in trouble with the police. It was found that 48 per cent of the drug-takers had five or more friends who had been in trouble with the police compared to only 10 per cent of the controls (difference significant at 1 per cent level).

The hypothesis was upheld as significantly more drug-takers had more than five friends who had been in trouble with the police.

These figures indicate that the drug-takers tend to belong to a more delinquent group of friends than do the controls, and that, as evidenced by the large number who have been in trouble with the police, they take an active part in the group's activities.

Spare time activities

LEISURE PURSUITS

Of all the leisure activities asked about, the following are those where significant differences were found between the two groups.

As can be seen from the table on page 120 the drug-takers spend less time than the controls with their family and spend more time with their peers at coffee bars, dancing, in pubs and in Soho. This supports hypothesis no. 18, which stated that the more times school children went to parties, coffee bars, pubs, Soho or dances against participating in alternative activities the more likely they were to take drugs. In fact the drug-takers spend a lot of their spare time in the very places where one would expect drugs to be available. This fact alone would perhaps account for why drug-takers know more than the controls about drugs and why they are more likely to be offered drugs than controls are. Again the

LEISURE PURSUITS OF DRUG-TAKERS AND CONTROLS (*percentages*)

Activity	Drug-takers	Controls	Level of significance
(*e*) go out with the rest of the family	7	34	1
(*h*) sit around in a coffee bar	46	7	1
(*i*) go to a pub	68	26	1
(*n*) go out with the girls	78	46	1
(*u*) go dancing	53	26	1
(*r*) go to Soho	19	4	5
(*s*) work on a motor car or bike	17	5	5
(*l*) sit at home with the rest of the family	44	61	10
(*o*) go out with the boys	69	51	10
(*q*) do a part time job	59	42	10
	$N=59$	59	

fact that the drug-takers spend less time with their family would support the earlier finding that drug-takers referred less often than their controls to their parents when they had a personal problem. It is perhaps interesting, though not surprising, that so many under-age children, still at school, frequent public houses.

PEER GROUP RELATIONSHIPS

Hypothesis no. 28 stated that the longer school children spend in peer groups the more likely they are to take drugs. It has already been seen above that the drug-takers go out with the girls and the boys more than the controls do. In a second question on this subject they were asked whom they usually went out with. Only one significant difference was found (10 per cent level of significance), which was that drug-takers more often than controls went out with a group of both boys and girls. It would therefore appear that the findings are in line with the hypothesis as the previous section shows that drug-takers spend less time with their family and more time going out with boys and girls than do the controls. What this finding, i.e. drug-takers more often go out in mixed company than do the controls, does, is to offer more support to the idea that the drug-takers' behaviour is more typical of older teenagers. This is because generally speaking mixed groups occur later in adolescence than do single sex groupings.

Another hypothesis, no. 27, in this section was that the more anxious school children are about peer group relationships the more likely they are to take drugs. A scale to measure this was included in Questionnaire B. A significant difference was found between the two groups, but in the opposite direction to that hypothesised, i.e. that in fact the drug-takers were less worried about peer group relationships than the controls ($p=0·0139$, significant at 5 per cent level). Though this fails to support the hypothesis (which was based mainly on American findings), it is in keeping with the previous findings which have suggested that the drug-takers spend more time with their peers than the controls.

Personality

The specific hypothesis tested here, no. 30, was that the greater the ego strength school children have the less likely they are to take drugs. This was tested by a short scale in Questionnaire B. No significant difference was found between the two groups ($p=0·4052$) and the hypothesis was therefore rejected. It must, however, be pointed out that the scale consisted of only six items and before this aspect of personality can be rejected outright as a determinant of school-child drug-taking, a more adequate personality test must be given. This finding though is not out of keeping with what is already known. The suggestion so far has been that the drug-takers' behaviour is typical of an older age group and this does not necessarily mean that they have inadequate personalities. If on the other hand it had been found that drug-takers more often than controls came from families where one or both parents were missing then it would have been surprising if no difference in personality had emerged.

Money

AMOUNT

Subjects were asked how much money they earned or were given each week. The result showed that 83 per cent of the drug-takers received or earned at least £1 a week compared to only 51 per cent of the controls (difference significant at 1 per cent level). The drug-takers therefore had significantly more money to spend each week. As more drug-takers than controls had part-time jobs, this might well have accounted for the difference.

PROPORTION SAVED

The hypothesis tested here, no. 23, was that the more school children save money the less likely they are to take drugs. When the subjects were asked what they did with their weekly money it was found that only 58 per cent of the drug-takers saved any of theirs compared to 83 per cent of the controls (significant at 1 per cent level). The hypothesis was therefore supported.

MONEY SPENT ON CLOTHES, CIGARETTES, ALCOHOL AND DRINK

Seventy-four per cent of the drug-takers spent some of their money on clothes compared to 56 per cent of the controls (significant at 5 per cent level). On the question of how much they spent on cigarettes, drugs and alcohol it was found that 78 per cent of the drug-takers compared to only 31 per cent of the controls (difference significant at 1 per cent level) spent some of their money in this way. In fact 39 per cent of the drug-takers spent at least half their weekly money on these commodities while the comparable figure for the controls was only 6 per cent.

It can therefore be seen that the drug-takers had more money to spend each than the controls and that whereas the controls were more likely to save their money the drug-takers were more likely to spend it on clothes, cigarettes, drink and drugs.

Smoking

As regards smoking, 79 per cent of the drug-takers said that they had smoked compared to only 29 per cent of the controls (difference significant at 1 per cent level).

Of those who smoked, the drug-takers were the heavier smokers: 68 per cent of the drug-takers who smoked took twenty or more cigarettes a week, while only 19 per cent of the controls who smoked used this amount. These two results support hypothesis no. 21, that the more school children smoke the more likely they are to take drugs. Whether one smoked or not appeared to be related to whether one's friends did, for when subjects were asked how many of their friends smoked when they were alone with them, it was found that 84 per cent of the drug-takers said half or more of theirs did compared to only 46 per cent of the controls (difference significant at 1 per cent level). This finding was supported by the fact that when asked how many boys and girls they knew who smoked, 46 per cent of the drug-takers said that they knew more than fifty, while only 15 per cent of the controls knew this number (difference significant at 1 per cent level).

Alcohol consumption

All of the drug-takers (100 per cent) had drunk alcohol other than at home compared to 76 per cent of the controls (difference significant at 1 per cent level). Of those who drank, the drug-takers did so more heavily than the controls. This was similar to the pattern for cigarette smoking. In fact 66 per cent of the drug-takers had a drink at least once a week compared to only 28 per cent of the controls who drank (difference significant at 1 per cent level). This finding was supported by the fact that though there was no difference among the subjects who had drunk beer and cider, significantly more of the drug-takers had drunk whisky, vodka and liqueurs when compared to the controls who drank. These findings support hypothesis no. 22, that the more school children drink the more likely they are to take drugs.

The similarity with cigarette smoking continues when one looks at how many of the subject's friends drank. Answers showed that 90 per cent of the drug-takers said half or more of their friends drank compared to 42 per cent of the controls (difference significant at 1 per cent level). Additional evidence for this finding comes from the fact that 47 per cent of the drug-takers knew fifty or more boys and girls who drank while only 12 per cent of the controls knew as many. So again it would appear that the circle of acquaintances in which a school child moves is related to the individual's particular behavioural patterns.

Number of drug-taking acquaintances

With drug-taking the same pattern as for alcohol and cigarettes emerges. Here when out with their friends only 2 per cent of the controls said that any of them took drugs. In contrast 48 per cent of the drug-takers said at least a quarter of their friends took drugs when they were out together, 9 per cent said that at least half of their friends did and one subject said that all of his friends took drugs when they were out together. The same pattern was repeated when subjects were asked how many boys and girls they knew who took drugs: 65 per cent of the drug-takers said that they knew six or more who took drugs while only 2 per cent of the controls knew this many. It is also important to note that at some time or other, 15 per cent of the controls said that they had been offered drugs and refused them.

These findings support two hypotheses on the availability of drugs: no. 8, that the more people school children know who have taken drugs the more likely they are to take drugs; and no. 9, that the more times school children have been in the company of other boys and girls who have taken drugs the more likely they are to take drugs.

It is interesting to note that whereas 46 per cent of the drug-takers knew fifty or more people who smoked and 47 per cent of them knew fifty or more boys and girls who drank, only 10 per cent of them knew more than fifty boys and girls who took drugs. Drug-taking is therefore an activity involving fewer people than cigarettes or alcohol and might well be the more 'daring' stage beyond these two.

At this stage there is already a general picture beginning to emerge. The drug-takers are more removed from their parents; they and their friends spend their leisure in different places from the controls, they have more money to spend, they are more likely to be delinquent and they smoke and drink more. In fact their behaviour is more typical of that of an older teenage group.

Job aspirations

The hypothesis tested here, no. 17, stated that school children with more upwardly mobile job aspirations are less likely to take drugs. A comparison was made between a subject's social class as determined by his father's occupation and the social class of the job he hoped to do once he had left school. There was no significant difference between the two groups and the hypothesis is therefore rejected.

Attitudes to life

These attitudes were tested in Questionnaire C by a series of paired statements where subjects were forced to choose one of each pair. There were seventeen of these paired statements. The answers to them are given below:

Attitudes to life of drug-takers and controls

| | % Agreeing | | |
Attitude	Drug-takers	Controls	$x =$ significant at 5% level
1 (a) A teenager should be liked by as many people as possible *or*	53	59	
(b) A teenager should not pay attention to what other people think	46	41	

Attitude to life of drug-takers and controls—*continued*

Attitude	% Agreeing Drug-takers	Controls	$x=$ significant at 5% level
2 (*a*) One should never get help from others with one's homework	62	62	
or			
(*b*) It doesn't matter who helps with one's homework as long as the teacher does not find out	38	38	
3 (*a*) If one finds a purse in the street one should always give it to a policeman	52	74	*x*
or			
(*b*) Anything one finds in the street one should be able to keep for oneself	48	26	*x*
4 (*a*) Life is too short to work	35	17	
or			
(*b*) Only foolish people do not work	65	83	*x*
5 (*a*) What I would most like to do is lead a useful life	47	68	*x*
or			
(*b*) What I would most like to do is earn lots of money	53	32	*x*
6 (*a*) The police often pick on us for no good reason	61	15	*x*
or			
(*b*) The police do a difficult job as well as they can	39	85	*x*

Attitude to life of drug-takers and controls—*continued*

| | % Agreeing | | |
Attitude	Drug-takers	Controls	$x =$ significant at 5% level
7 (*a*) Nothing can stop me when I make up my mind to do something	61	39	*x*
or			
(*b*) I always hesitate and listen to others before doing anything	39	61	*x*
8 (*a*) There is a lot of truth in what the Church says	33	48	
or			
(*b*) Church is a waste of time	67	52	
9 (*a*) Only squares are always on time	9	12	
or			
(*b*) A person should always be on time	91	88	
10 (*a*) Life is more fun when one does daring things	58	49	
or			
(*b*) One should always be sure something is safe before one does it	42	51	
11 (*a*) Any homework should always be done as best you can do it	67	71	
or			
(*b*) As long as the teacher says the homework is all right it does not matter how good you think it is	33	29	
12 (*a*) One should never work too hard	42	35	
or			
(*b*) Hard work can be a lot of fun	58	65	

Attitude to life of drug-takers and controls—*continued*

Attitude	Drug-takers	Controls	$x =$ significant at 5% level
	% Agreeing		
13 (a) A teenager should always try something new	98	97	
or			
(b) A teenager should stick to the old and trusted ways	2	3	
14 (a) One should pay attention to those older than yourself	40	51	
or			
(b) Young people know that older people are often wrong	60	49	
15 (a) One should never steal anything	60	80	x
or			
(b) Sometimes it is all right to steal	40	20	x
16 (a) The best job is one that pays a lot of money	70	70	
or			
(b) The best job to have is where one can draw or write	30	30	
17 (a) The best thing to do is to live as if today was the last day one had to live	33	13	x
or			
(b) One should always plan for the future	67	87	x

Two hypotheses were tested in this section. The first, no. 24, said that the more school children repudiated middle-class norms, as defined primarily by A. K. Cohen (48:88–91), the more likely they were to take drugs. Obviously in a short scale it is not possible to examine a complete range of values. Among the norms of middle-class behaviour given by Cohen which were looked at here were: a readiness to postpone immediate gratification, respect for property, individual responsibility and the cultivation of manners. In respect to the first of these, answers to question 17 showed that significantly more drug-takers believed that one should live as if today was the last day one had. Similarly, in answer to question 7, significantly more drug-takers believed that nothing could stop them when they had made up their mind to do something. On the two questions which dealt with property, questions 3 and 15, significantly more drug-takers believed that it was all right to steal. Question 6, which deals with attitudes to police, is also relevant here and it is interesting to note that significantly fewer drug-takers believed that police did a difficult job as well as they could. Individual responsibility was measured by questions 1, 2 and 11. No significant difference was found between the two groups. Question 9 was concerned with the cultivation of manners; no significant difference was found.

Other values which questions were aimed at testing were: belief in established religion, question 8; belief in being daring, questions 10 and 13; belief in respect for elders, question 14 and finally belief in the value of work, questions 4 and 16. In all of these cases, except for one part of question 4, no significant differences were found between the two groups. Therefore as regards only two norms of behaviour could it be said that drug-takers repudiate middle-class values. Therefore the hypothesis is only marginally supported and this area needs further investigation with a more detailed questionnaire.

The second hypothesis, no. 25, stated that the more emphasis school children place on material as against other life goals the more likely they are to take drugs. The answers to questions 5 and 16 were relevant to this hypothesis. In question 5 significantly more drug-takers wanted to earn money rather than lead a useful life. However, in question 16 there was no difference between the two groups. The two questions though are not strictly comparable and to agree with one item in one of the pairs does not imply a necessity to agree with the same item in another pair. The two questions are not therefore of sufficient depth to enable one to either reject or accept the hypothesis.

Attitudes to drugs

TOTAL ATTITUDE SCORE

The hypothesis tested, no. 26, said that the more favourable the attitudes towards drug-taking that school children hold the more likely they are to take drugs. A total score was obtained for each subject on the Likert scale measuring attitudes to drugs (Questionnaire G), and the scores for members of each group were then compared and tested for significance by the Wilcoxon Matched-Pairs Signed-Ranks test. This yielded a z score of 4·99, $p = 0·00003$, significant at the 1 per cent level. The null hypothesis that there is no significant difference between the two groups is therefore rejected and the hypothesis that drug-takers have the more favourable attitudes to drugs is accepted.

COMPARISON ON INDIVIDUAL ITEMS

A further analysis was carried out on this questionnaire in which the drug-takers and controls were compared on each of the items included. This was to see if there were any significant differences on any of the specific opinions about drugs that collectively made up the total scale. The percentage of each of the two groups which agreed with each of the items is given below. In the final column the percentage of all the non-drug-takers ($N = 1031$) agreeing with each item is given.

ATTITUDES TO DRUGS BY DRUG-TAKERS AND CONTROLS

Attitude	Drug-takers	Controls	$x =$ significant at 5% level	All non-drug-takers
1 Drugs are all right if only taken occasionally	61·2	16·9	x	17
2 Drugs are an aid to creative people	58·0	20·4	x	28
3 You can't trust drug-takers	42·8	54·4		50
4 Drugs are not as dangerous as newspapers make out	61·8	20·4	x	18
5 Drugs can make you a fuller person	44·2	13·6	x	12

ATTITUDES TO DRUGS BY DRUG-TAKERS AND CONTROLS
—*continued*

Attitude	Drug-takers	Controls	$x =$ significant at 5% level	All non-drug-takers
6 Smoking is more dangerous than taking drugs	11·8	6·8		7
7 Only if you take drugs can you make the London scene	6·8	5·1		4
8 Drugs will make you mad	28·9	25·1		37
9 Not enough is known about drugs to make them safe	64·4	79·8		69
10 It is safer to drive with someone high on pot rather than with someone drunk on alcohol	42·4	8·5	x	16
11 Drugs are good because they make you self-confident	45·7	8·5	x	10
12 The risk of heroin hooking you is over exaggerated	25·4	10·2	x	12
13 It would be fine to take drugs if it were not for the police	30·5	1·7	x	7
14 Drugs are a valuable new experience	55·9	20·4	x	17
15 Only fools get hooked on drugs	32·3	57·7	x	64
16 Pep pills are great for kicks	54·5	5·1	x	11
17 Drugs are all right if one doesn't take alcohol at the same time	40·8	8·5	x	10

On twelve of the seventeen items there was a significant difference between the drug-takers and the controls.

Drug knowledge

The specific hypothesis tested here, no. 10, was that the more knowledge about drugs that someone has the more likely they are to have taken drugs. This was tested by Questionnaire F, in two parts. The first consisted of knowledge about different drugs and the second part was concerned with drug terminology. The questionnaire was scored in three ways. A score was obtained for each part and also a total score was given for subjects. On all three scores there was a significant difference between the two groups (at the 1 per cent level). The hypothesis was therefore accepted.

In a further analysis the answers of the total sample were found for each of the individual questions in the first part of the questionnaire. These are given below.

ANSWERS OF TOTAL SAMPLE TO DRUG KNOWLEDGE QUESTIONS (*indicates the right answer)

	Percentage answering each question ($N=1089$)			
	True	False	Don't know	N.A.
1 The only way one can take LSD is on a sugar lump	5	49*	46	0·6
2 Marijuana is made from the same plant as heroin	14	25*	60	0·9
3 Heroin costs about 20s a grain on the black market	19*	12	69	1
4 Tolerance means that one comes to like a drug the more one takes it	21	34*	43	2
5 Many adults are dependent upon barbiturates	29*	16	54	2
6 LSD tastes like milk	2	14*	83	2
7 Pep pills help to keep you awake	53*	10	35	2

ANSWERS OF TOTAL SAMPLE TO DRUG KNOWLEDGE
QUESTIONS—*continued*

	Percentage answering each question ($N = 1089$)			
	True	False	Don't know	N.A.
8 Withdrawal symptoms come when one takes too big a dose of a drug	28	15*	56	2
9 LSD always gives one hallucinations	45	11*	43	1
10 A reefer is cheaper to buy than a grain of heroin	30*	6	63	1
11 Everyone always gets the same effects from a drug	6	62*	31	1
12 Heroin at first often makes you sick	26*	4	69	1
13 LSD is the only known psychedelic drug	13	32*	54	1
14 As soon as one has some heroin one is hooked on it	20	42*	37	1
15 Physical addiction means that one's body comes to need the drug	65*	5	28	2
16 LSD has the same effect every time it is taken	10	46*	43	1
17 Beginners do not always enjoy marijuana	27*	6	65	2
18 No pep pills are addictive	10	39*	50	1
19 Marijuana and hashish are different preparations from the same plant	21*	10	68	1
20 The only way one can take heroin is by injecting it	26	21*	52	1
21 One can take as many pep pills as one likes with no ill effects	3	63*	33	1
22 Marijuana can be cooked and eaten as a sweetmeat	8*	16	75	1

ANSWERS OF TOTAL SAMPLE TO DRUG KNOWLEDGE
QUESTIONS—*continued*

	Percentage answering each question ($N = 1089$)			
	True	False	Don't know	N.A.
23 Heroin is never taken in combination with any other drug	15	16*	67	2
24 Mescaline is another name for marijuana	4	12*	81	2
25 Once you start taking pep pills you can't stop	17	46*	36	1
26 LSD was first manufactured in Switzerland	11*	12	76	2
27 Cigarettes and alcohol are drugs	64*	21	14	2
28 Marijuana usually effects you so much that other people might think you were mad	32	14*	54	1
29 'Four and four' is a term used by doctors when referring to the number of male and female addicts	4	9*	85	2
30 Immediately one takes LSD spectacular things happen	24	22*	53	2
31 Drug dependency means that one's life is centred around drugs	60*	5	34	1
32 Marijuana is used by a large number of G.P.s to make patients well	20	18*	61	1
33 No one can tell by any means whatever whether you have taken a pep pill or not	9	49*	40	2
34 Hashish is normally cut up and smoked	46*	5	46	3
35 All pep pills look the same	6	47*	46	2
36 Once you start taking heroin regularly you keep needing more and more to get any kick	63*	3	32	2

ANSWERS OF TOTAL SAMPLE TO DRUG KNOWLEDGE
QUESTIONS—*continued*

	Percentage answering each question ($N = 1089$)			
	True	False	Don't know	N.A.
37 Marijuana is made from the same plant as hashish	20*	6	73	2
38 A heroin taker often starts off with a one-sixth of a grain	10*	5	83	2
39 Cannabis looks more like LSD than marijuana	5	11*	82	2
40 Phyceptone is addictive	6*	5	87	2
41 Amphetamines do not have the same effect as barbiturates	13*	7	78	2
42 Like anything else, one needs a lot of LSD before it has any effect	8	38*	52	1
43 Psilocybin is a pep pill	6	5*	87	2
44 Heroin is grown on a heroin tree	3	44*	51	2
45 LSD is colourless, tasteless and odourless	21*	9	66	3
46 Marijuana can only be taken by injection	7	35*	53	5

In only 7 out of the 46 items over 50 per cent of the sample gave the right answer. This indicates that there is a lack of knowledge about drugs among school children. However, in only 4 of the questions did more than 25 per cent of the subjects give the wrong answer. Therefore, even though there might be an absence of accurate knowledge about drugs among school children there is also an absence of inaccurate knowledge.

Perception of self, ideal self and drug-takers

Three separate questionnaires (D, E and H) were used to measure these three concepts. The aim was to see if the drug-takers and the controls had different perceptions of people who took drugs in relation to the perceptions they held of themselves. In analysing the answers the subjects' score on each item in all three scales were combined and the total scores for all of the subjects in the drug-taker and control groups were then factor analysed. Six first order factors with a latent root > 1 were extracted. The first four of these, which accounted for 46 per cent of the total variance, proved meaningful. They are given below with the items which had a loading of at least 0·40.

FACTOR 1

ITEM

		Loading
3	Not good at sports	− ·56
10	Have 1 or 2 friends	·61
11	Neat and clean	·76
15	Do not swear	·51
16	Save money	·50

This factor was interpreted as measuring conventionality.

FACTOR 2

ITEM

		Loading
1	Not good at school work	− ·44
4	Tough	− ·66
6	Like to be with a group	− ·65
12	Do not bully	·43
19	Tough	− ·69

This factor was interpreted as measuring weakness.

FACTOR 3

ITEM

		Loading
5	Usually do as I am told	− ·75
8	Act my own age	− ·49
9	Cannot wait, want everything at once	·75
10	Do not do forbidden things	− ·62

This factor was interpreted as measuring an obendiece-disobedience dimension.

Kᴅꜱ

FACTOR 4

ITEM

	Loading
2 Not interested in the opposite sex	·80
10 Have 1 or 2 friends	·44
18 Do not attract opposite sex	·81

This factor appeared to be measuring heterosexual appeal.

In the next step a score was obtained for each individual for each factor in each concept. That is, a score was obtained for each individual on how he saw drug-takers, ideal self and self in terms of conventionality, weakness, obedience and heterosexual appeal. This score was obtained by summing the individuals' answers to the items which had a loading of 0·40 or more on each factor. Each answer was given an equal weight. That is that on factor four, for example, the subject's answers to items 2, 10 and 18 in each of the three questionnaires were added together and this gave the subject's score on that factor for each of the concepts.

The next step was to see if there were any differences between how the drug-takers and the controls perceived the relationship of the concepts of self, ideal self and people who take drugs in each of the four factors. To test this a Friedman Two-Way Analysis of Variance was carried out between the scores of each group on the three concepts for each factor. For example, on the factor of conventionality the scores of the drug-takers on the concepts of self, ideal self and people who take drugs were tested to see if there was any significant differences between the three concepts. If a significant difference was found then each pair of scores was compared by the Wilcoxon Matched-Pairs Signed-Ranks Test, i.e. the drug-takers' image of the self on the factor of conventionality was compared to the drug-takers' image of the ideal self and afterwards to the drug-takers' image of the people who take drugs.

The results of this analysis were that on the factor of conventionality both the drug-takers and the controls perceived people who take drugs to be significantly less conventional than they perceived themselves to be. Both groups also perceived themselves to be significantly less conventional than they perceived their ideal selves to be.

On the second factor of weakness, while the controls perceived people who take drugs to be significantly tougher than they saw themselves to be, the drug-takers saw no significant difference between how they perceived themselves and how they perceived people who take drugs. While the drug-takers perceived their ideal self as being less tough than they perceived themselves, the controls saw no difference between their perception of themselves and their perception of their ideal self.

On the third factor of obedience both the drug-takers and the controls perceived people who take drugs to be significantly more disobedient than they perceived themselves to be. However, while the drug-takers perceived themselves to be significantly more disobedient than their ideal selves, there was no significant difference in how the controls perceived themselves and their ideal selves.

On the fourth factor of heterosexual appeal there was no significant difference in how the controls perceived themselves, their ideal selves and the people who take drugs. The drug-takers, however, saw people who take drugs as having more heterosexual appeal than they perceived themselves to have, though there was no difference between their perception of their self and their ideal self on this factor.

These findings are probably easier to understand if presented diagrammatically as below:

FACTOR 1 Conventionality

(a) Ideal self —————[1] Self —————People who take drugs (D.T.)[2]
        Conventional (← →) Unconventional
(b) Ideal self ————— Self ————— People who take Drugs (C)[3]

FACTOR 2 Weakness

(c) Ideal self ————— Self
                People who take drugs (D.T.)
      Weak (← →) Tough
(d) Ideal self
         ————— Drug-taker (C)
      Self

---

[1] ————— = significant differences at least at 5 per cent level.
[2] D.T. = How controls perceive the relation of the three concepts.
[3] C = How controls perceive the relation of the three concepts.

FACTOR 3 Obedience
(*e*) Ideal self ----- Self ----- People who take drugs (D.T.
       Obedient (← →) Disobedient
(*f*) Ideal Self
     ----- People who take drugs (C)
     Self

FACTOR 4 Heterosexual appeal
(*g*) Self
     ----- People who take drugs (D.T.)
  Ideal self
  Little heterosexual appeal (← →) heterosexual appeal
(*h*) Ideal self
    Self (C)
  People who take drugs

This section was testing three hypotheses:

no. 11, the greater the similarity between the perception of the ideal self and that of the drug-taker the more likely one is to take drugs;

no. 12, the greater the similarity between the self and the ideal self and the greater their discrepancy with the perception of the drug taker the less likely one is to take drugs;

no. 13, the greater the similarity between the perception of the self and the perception of a drug-taker the more likely one is to take drugs.

These hypotheses can also be presented diagrammatically:

no. 11   Ideal self
       People who take drugs
no. 12   Self
        ----- People who take drugs
       Ideal Self
no. 13   Self
       People who take drugs

In operational terms one would expect:

(a) that in hypothesis 11 there would be no significant difference between how the drug-takers perceived their ideal self
and how they perceived people who take drugs. In contrast
one would expect that in the case of controls there would be
a significant difference in between how they perceived their
ideal self and how they perceived people who take drugs.

(b) that in hypothesis 12 there would be no significant
difference between how drug-takers perceived themselves
and how they perceived their ideal selves and that there
would be no significant difference between these two perceptions and how drug-takers perceived people who took
drugs. In the case of the controls one would expect that there
would be a significant difference between their self and ideal
self images and that of people who take drugs.

(c) that in hypothesis 13 for drug-takers there would be no
significant difference between their perception of themselves
and their perception of people who take drugs. In the case
of the controls one would expect there to be a difference
between their self perception and that of people who take
drugs.

Hypothesis 11. If one now refers to the diagrammatic representation of the results one can see that in factor 1 the perceptions
of the drug-takers contradict the hypothesis while those of the
controls support it. A similar pattern emerges in factors 2 and 3.
In factor 4 the perceptions of both groups contradict the hypothesis.

Hypothesis 12. In all four factors the perceptions of the drug-
takers contradict the hypothesis. In factors 1 and 4 the results of
the controls contradict the hypothesis but in the case of factors 2
and 3 the results for the controls are in line with what was
hypothesised.

Hypothesis 13. In factor 1 the perceptions of the control subjects
support the hypothesis while those of the drug-takers contradict
it. In factor 2 both sets of figures support the hypothesis. In
factor 3 the perceptions of the control subjects support the hypothesis while those of the drug-takers contradict it and finally in
factor 4 both sets of findings fail to support the hypothesis.

It can therefore be seen that the support for the three hypotheses is most tentative and what support there is tends to come from the findings of the controls. The implication of this is that in most cases the drug-takers do not identify themselves with the people who take drugs. In fact when the self images of the drug-takers and the controls were compared on the four factors the only significant difference between the two groups was on the factor of disobedience where the drug-takers perceived themselves to be more disobedient than the controls.

Sentence completion items (*general*)

The answers to questions 2, 4 and 5, Questionnaire I, will be discussed in the next section.

1 *I am most nervous:* The answers here were too varied to be coded meaningfully.

3 *To be tolerant* . . .: Most answers from both groups either defined the word with varying degrees of accuracy or agreed that tolerance was a good thing. Further analysis did not appear to be fruitful.

6 *I think the world will end in* . . . .: The answers were categorised as follows:

	World will end in 200 years or less	World will end in war or chaos	Other
Drug-takers: $N=$	7	7	45
Controls: $N=$	6	7	46

It had been thought that a feeling of despondency about the world's future might be a reason for taking drugs. At this level, however, this does not seem to be the case. It is perhaps interesting to note that 27 out of 118 subjects (23 per cent) had what could be called a pessimistic outlook for the world's future. This is in line with the figures for the total sample where out of 712 completed answers to this question, 214 (30 per cent) predicted the world would either end in less than 200 years or in war or chaos.

7 *I think that it is likely in the future . . .:* The pattern here was similar to that for question 6:

	Answers mentioning drugs	Answers predicting war	Answers predicting end of world	Other
Drug-takers: N=	9	3	4	43
Controls: N=	5	4	3	43

8 *I wish my friends would . . . .:* The answers were so varied that no meaningful categorisation was possible.

Sentence completion items (*Questionnaire I, drug questions*)

In this and the next section, the drug-takers' answers are compared to the answers of all the non-drug-takers.

QUESTIONS 2 AND 5

1 *Drug-takers' answer to question 2: The first time I took drugs . . .:* Out of the 59 drug-takers, 52 answered this question. Their answers can be divided into the categories of when, where, why and what effect. Some answers contain parts appropriate to more than one category and where this happens the answer was sub-divided so that the relevant parts appear in the relevant category.

When
Fourteen subjects gave answers which indicated what their age was when they first took drugs.

AGE WHEN FIRST DRUG TAKEN

	Sex		
Age	Male	Female	Total
13	1	—	1
14	4	2	6
15	3	2	5
16	1	1	2

Of these fourteen subjects, thirteen were occasional users.

Where

Eleven of the subjects gave answers which indicated where they were when they first took drugs.

4 mentioned that they were at a club
3 mentioned that they were at a friend's house
2 mentioned that they were at a party
1 mentioned that he was at his own house alone
1 mentioned that he was beside Regent's Park.

Why

Nine subjects indicated the reason why they took the drug. As eight of these are different, they are listed below:

—was just for a laugh
—it was only experimental. I have not taken any since
—and stayed up all night dancing
—I was a stupid little baby
—my boyfriend . . . and he told me to take one so I did
—and did it for the sake of it
—I thought I was being clever and did not want to miss anything
—was when mentally depressed
—I was depressed.

Effect

The effect of the drug on the first occasion was mentioned in 28 of the answers. For thirteen, information was also available as to the drug that was used.

Type of drug used	Favourable effect	Unfavourable effect	No effect
Pep pills	2	2	1
Hashish	1	5	1
LSD	1		

The numbers are too small for any significant differences to be found but the table appears to indicate that one is more likely to have an unfavourable reaction to cannabis rather than to pep pills. The complete 28 answers are given below:

'I felt sick afterwards but I still took some more when I got used to them' (occasional user)[1]

'It gave me a headache' (occasional user: pep pills)

'I felt very sick and wished I had never touched it' (occasional user: hashish)

'Bloody tasted like ferkin curry' (occasional user: pep pills)

'I did not like it and was sick the next day' (occasional user: hashish)

'I got one hell of a kick out of them' (occasional user: pep pills)

'They had no effect' (occasional user)

'I flipped' (regular user: hashish)

'It was too much I felt great' (regular user)

'I didn't get high and have never taken them since' (occasional user: pep pills)

'I had a marvellous time' (regular user)

'I felt awful the next morning' (regular user)

'I was excited' (occasional user: LSD)

'I felt greater' (occasional user: pep pills)

'I thought I was blooming mad' (occasional user: hashish)

'I was shocked' (occasional user)

'It was all right until about 3.0 a.m. when I saw people on a record sleeve attack me' (occasional user)

'I experienced a new perception of life' (occasional user)

'I thought it was great and I was really having a rave time' (regular user)

'I was very ill' (regular user)

'I was sick' (regular user: hashish)

'It had virtually no effect apart from a little tiredness' (occasional user: hashish)

'I kept awake that night but was very tired and depressed the next day' (occasional user)

'I enjoyed them' (regular user)

'I almost vomited' (regular user)

---

[1] Degree of drug use and drug first used are given where known.

'. . . but now having tried them I am no longer certain that they provide any great risk' (occasional user)

'I didn't notice much but a headache' (occasional user: hashish)

'I felt above it all. Everything was so fast yet a bit of a drag' (regular user)

'I felt great' (occasional user)

2 *Drug-takers' answers to question 5: Looking back on all the times I have taken drugs I think:* The drug-takers' answers to this question were divided into four groups as follows:

Experience worth having	15
Experience not worth having	19
A good experience while they lasted	5
No particular effect/answer irrelevant	7
	——
	46
	——

3 *Non-drug-takers' answers to question 2:* As has already been mentioned, 153 subjects who were classified as non-drug-takers gave meaningful answers to question 2. It is interesting to divide these answers into the same categories as those for the drug-takers.

When
No answers fitted here.

Where
Six answers were appropriate. Four subjects said that the first occasion occurred at a party, one said on holiday and one said in Soho.

Why
Six answers indicated why the subject took drugs on the first occasion. Four of these mentioned peer group pressure, one said it was a good idea and the other said it was 'because I was not attractive to the opposite sex'.

Effect
One hundred and two answers dealt with the effect. Only 24 of these said that they were favourable.

4 *Non-drug-takers' answers to question 5:* One hundred and sixty-one subjects answered this question. All but five of the answers could be categorised into whether the drug experience was worth while or not worth while. Of these 156, 140 (90 per cent) were categorised as being not worth while.

9 *Estimation of the number of drug-takers within a school*

This question was added to the end of the questionnaires for subjects in the second sample to see if it was possible to check the number of drug-takers within a school by getting the subjects themselves to estimate the number of drug-takers. Though the question also included estimates of the numbers who smoked and drank, there was no point in analysing these as both of these activities would be indulged in by children in pre-school-leaving years as well as by those in the school-leaving years on which the survey concentrated. As far as drug-taking was concerned it seemed likely that this would be concentrated in the school-leaving years.

The estimates can be divided into those given by the non-drug-takers and those given by the drug-takers themselves. As regards the former there was a certain amount of agreement:

School 7. Of 61 codeable answers, 70·5 per cent estimated that fewer than 25 pupils in the school took drugs. Survey found nine drug-takers.

School 8. Of 77 answers, 69 per cent estimated that fewer than 25 pupils in the school took drugs. The survey found 10.

School 9. Of 66 answers, 84 per cent estimated that fewer than 25 pupils took drugs. The survey found 6, but it only included the fourth form.

There is nowhere near as much agreement among the estimates of the drug-takers.

School 7. Three estimated there were fewer than 6 drug-takers, one estimated 6–10, four gave the number as 21–25.

School 8. Two estimated 6–10, one each gave 16–20, 31–40, 41–50, two gave 71–80, one gave 81–90 and two again over 150.

School 9. Estimates were one each for the figures between 6–10, 16–20, 21–25, 41–50, 81–90, and 100–120.

In retrospect this divergence among the drug-takers is not so surprising. First, as drug-taking can start as young as fourteen or fifteen the survey might have excluded some drug-takers. Secondly, as forty-four of the fifty-nine drug-takers were occasional users their drug-taking experience might all have been with non-school peers. Thirdly, children are likely to boast about their experiences, and fourthly, in any school cliques exist and members do not necessarily have accurate knowledge about the behaviour of members of other cliques. A final reason might well be that drug-takers tend to project their behaviour on to others.

This additional question therefore proved to have only limited utility. In so far as the survey had indicated that the problem in each school was confined to a minority of the subjects, it was useful that the estimates of the non-drug-takers in each school accorded with this. However, in terms of hoping to obtain by these estimates an accurate figure of the number of drug-takers within the schools, the question was obviously inadequate.

FURTHER ANALYSES

Comments, drug names and drug knowledge for the total sample:

COMMENTS

In the first part of the sample the subjects who finished first were asked to write their comments about the survey on the back of the questionnaire. A provisional examination of these indicated that the subjects had important things to say about various aspects of the survey. A question, asking for comments, was therefore added to the end of the questionnaires for subjects in the second part of the sample. Altogether 577 out of the 1093 subjects commented on the questionnaires. In the first part of the sample the figures were 328 out of 794 (i.e. 41 per cent) and in the second part 249 out of 299 (83 per cent).

1 *Confidentiality*. Thirteen subjects commented on the confidentiality of the questionnaires. A typical comment was: 'I think a good point about this is the not naming of the paper as this helps people to answer truthfully.' Though the number of comments on this topic is small it does appear that for some subjects, confidentiality is an aid in answering truthfully.

2 *Questionnaire disguise.* As has already been mentioned, the subjects were never told the real purpose of the questionnaire and many of the important questions about drugs were sandwiched between similar questions on smoking and drinking. It was reassuring to find that only thirteen (2 per cent) of the 577 comments realised that the survey was primarily interested in those who took drugs. A typical comment in this category was: 'I think this questionnaire was merely an insight into our personal lives and how we lived them. It is also a way and means of detecting all the teenage drug addicts in the school, because so much time was concentrated upon drugs.'

In fact as will be seen below the majority of subjects thought the questionnaire was about general social problems with too much emphasis on drugs.

3 *Favourability of the comments.* The comments were divided into those that were favourable about the questionnaire, those that were unfavourable and others.

Favourable	262
Unfavourable	265
Other	24
Confidential	13
Disguise	13
	577

A typical answer in the 'other' category was: 'More tolerance should be given to younger people and they should have more respect even when half of them believe that they are God. By the way Jesus was a bastard liberally speaking. I do not believe in religion (except mine). Prayers will be answered by phone.'

Both the favourable and unfavourable comments were further subdivided:

Favourable		Unfavourable	
(i) Favourable without other comments	118	(viii) Unfavourable without other comment	60
(ii) Favourable but too much emphasis on drugs	84	(ix) Unfavourable because too much	

(iii) Favourable because of phrasing of some questions	25	emphasis upon drugs	122
(iv) Favourable because of interest in the person	15	(x) Unfavourable because of way some questions phrased	55
(v) Favourable except questions too personal	6	(xi) Unfavourable because questions too personal	8
(vi) Favourable but in parts boring	1	(xii) Other	20
(vii) Other	13		265
	262		

Below are examples from the categories above:

(i) 'This sort of thing helps people to be able to understand others and on the whole is a good thing.'

(ii) 'I think this is a new way of finding out more about the way young people's minds work. It is very good but there is too much here on drugs and most of us don't ever know the slightest thing about it.'

(iii) 'It was a very sensible form fill out, and it was very interesting to fill in. I do not mind these sorts of questions. I think that the widest range of questions possible has been confined very sensibly in this short form.'

(iv) 'It's good to do because it tells you about yourself and helps other people in a job they are also very interesting things to do.'

(v) 'Some of the questions I thought a bit too personal. Such as the money you earned and what job your father does. But on the whole I thought it was quite good and interesting.'

(vi) 'The questionnaire assumed too much that teenagers were scruffy hooligans who hang about on street corners stuffing themselves with drugs. Because of this I think that most of the people who compiled it are behind the times and believe everything that they read in newspapers and they ought to get off their pedestals and out of their Rolls Royces.'

(vii) 'I don't think it is fair to have all them questions about drugs because half of us don't no anything about them.'

(ix) 'I don't think it was quite frank enough, and could have asked us other things to which we wouldn't have reacted quite in a way that you might think.'

One final point is that of the 59 drug-takers, 39 gave comments, of which 23 were unfavourable and fourteen were favourable.

DRUG NAMES

Whereas in the pilot survey the number of additional colloquial drug names that subjects gave seemed to be an indication of whether a person took drugs or not, this did not apply here. Only 52 subjects gave names which had not appeared earlier in the questionnaire, and, of these, only eight were drug-takers.

Another purpose of question 4 in Questionnaire I, was to elicit the names by which various drugs were known by the subjects. In this the question was more successful as 59 names were given. Some of these, like 'horse' for heroin are well known but others, like 'weeps', did not seem to have been recorded before. The full list is given below. Where possible the type of drug to which the expression refers is given after each colloquial name (A=amphetamine, C=cannabis, L=LSD, H=heroin), though, because of the way the question is phrased, it has not always been possible to determine this. It might also be the case that some names have been invented at random.

The specific question asked was: 'Drugs are called by many different names, some of these are...' The answers are given below. The names also include those given in the pilot sample which were not mentioned again in this study; these are indicated by an asterisk.

NAMES OF DRUGS

B	F	L
Big H (H)	flodds ( )	leaf ( )
blue diamond (A)	fluffy ( )	light ( )
blues (A)	flusher ( )	lime juice ( )
bread (money)	French Blues (A)	
bombers (A)	Frenchies	M
blocks (A)	fruit ( )	misty ( )
beans (A)	fuzz (police)	Mary Jane (C)
bubbly bubbly ( )		mellow yellow ( )

NAMES OF DRUGS—*continued*

C	G	N
charge (C)	grass (C)	noddy ( )
charlie (cocaine)	gear (~~belongings~~) DRUGS	
* coke and pep (cocaine)		
	H	**P**
D	H (H)	pellet ( )
dobs/doubs/dubs (A)	heart ( )	Paris Blues (A)
dubes/dobes/dolbs	happening ( )	Paris nights (A)
dream ( )	horse (H)	pumps
digs (A)		
dubble blues (A)		**R**
dolls (A)		red devils (A)
dix ( )	**J**	
	jabs ( )	**S**
T	joint (C)	shit (**C**)
the stuff ( )	junk (H)	sky rider
thrills ( )		smoke (C)
tickets ( )	**W**	speed (A)
trip (L)	weeps	splits ( )
		swingers ( )
		stuff (H)

Subgroups

Ideally subsequent analysis of the data would involve the comparison of subgroups within the drug-taking population, e.g. male regular drug-takers of social class 1 and 2 versus male regular drug-takers of social classes 3 to 7 in order to see if there was any difference on a number of factors between regular drug-takers of one class and those of another. However, this breakdown would have meant comparing six subjects in one group with three in the other. These numbers are too small for meaningful analysis. The small number of drug-takers therefore restricts the possibilities for further analyses of the data.

What has been done is to take three subdivisions which appear to be most important, i.e. regular *v.* occasional users, delinquent *v.* non-delinquent users and male *v.* female drug users and to compare the two groups in each instance on the items in the questionnaires where relevant differences might be expected to appear.

(*a*) REGULAR *v.* OCCASIONAL USERS

As it has already been shown there were 44 occasional users and fifteen regular drug users in the sample.

Age. There was no significant difference between the two groups:

	Regular (%)	Occasional (%)
14/15	53	48
16 or over	47	52

Absent father. 20 per cent of the regular users and 18 per cent of the occasional users indicated that their father did not live in their home.

Position in school. 47 per cent of the regular users said they were in the top ten and 30 per cent of the occasional users also said they were. There was no significant difference between the two groups.

Delinquency. 67 per cent of the regular users and 54·5 per cent of the occasional users had been in trouble with the police. No significant difference was found between the two groups.

Spare time activities. The only significant difference here was that only 13 per cent of the regular users sat at home with the rest of the family at least once a week compared to 53·5 per cent of the occasional users.

Smoking. Significantly more regular users smoked cigarettes than did the occasional users: 100 per cent to 73 per cent (significant at 1 per cent level). Of those who smoked the regular users were the heavier smokers. 87 per cent of the regular users smoked 20 or more cigarettes a week compared to 59 per cent of the occasional users who smoked (significant at 5 per cent level).

Drinking. All the drug-takers had drunk alcohol and there was no significant difference between the two groups as regards their frequency of drinking.

Number of drug-taking acquaintances. Though there was no difference between the two groups as regards the number of their friends who would take drugs when they were alone with them, regular users knew significantly more boys and girls who took drugs than the occasional users: 87 per cent of the regular users knew six or more drug-takers compared to 59 per cent of the occasional users (difference significant of 5 per cent level).

Attitudes to drugs. The Mann Witney U test was applied to the scores of the two groups on the scale measuring attitudes to drugs. It was hypothesised that the regular drug-takers would have more favourable attitudes. A significant difference was found between the two groups ($z=1·87$, $p=0·0307$, significant at 5 per cent level) and the hypothesis was therefore supported.

LDS

Drug knowledge. The Mann Witney U test was again used and this time no significant difference was found between the two groups ($z = 1 \cdot 33$, $p = 0 \cdot 0918$) though the regular drug users had a higher score than the occasional users.

Relation of first drug experience to subsequent use. A further analysis was carried out on question 2 in Questionnaire I in order to see if the effect of the first drug experience had any effect on whether a person became a regular user.

EFFECT OF FIRST DRUG EXPERIENCE

	Favourable	Unfavourable	No effect	No answer
Regular users N =	6	6		3
Occasional users N =	4	9	3	

The unfavourable and no effect categories were combined to make a 2 × 2 table and a chi-square test was carried out but no significant difference was found ($\chi^2 = 1 \cdot 2$, $p = 0 \cdot 20$).

As can be seen from these limited comparisons the regular drug-takers differ only slightly from the occasional users and when they do differ it is because their behaviour is just that step beyond that of the occasional users, i.e. they spend less time with their family, they smoke more and also know more people who take drugs and as might be expected have more favourable attitudes about drugs.

(b) DELINQUENT *v.* NON-DELINQUENT USERS

Regular v. occasional users. There were 34 delinquent (i.e. subjects who said they had been in trouble with the police) drug-takers and 25 non-delinquent drug-takers; 29 per cent of the delinquent drug-takers (N = 10) were regular users compared to 20 per cent (N = 5) of the non-delinquent drug-takers. There was no significant difference between the two groups.

Number of friends in trouble with the police. The delinquents had significantly more friends who had been in trouble with the police than did the non-delinquents, i.e. 62 per cent of the delinquents had five or more friends who had been in trouble with the police compared to 28 per cent of the non-delinquents who knew this number (difference significant at 5 per cent level).

As regards the aim of this survey these are the two most relevant delinquency figures. They indicate first that whereas delinquency is associated with drug-taking in general among school children it is not associated with whether subjects are occasional or regular drug users.

Secondly, they indicate that whether one is delinquent or not is related to the number of delinquent people that one knows. This reinforces the pattern established earlier that drug-takers say they know more drug-takers than non-drug-takers do and serves to stress that the behavioural tendencies of one's peer group appear to be an important factor in determining an individual's behaviour.

(c) MALE v. FEMALE DRUG-TAKERS

There were thirty-seven male drug-takers and twenty-two female drug-takers and this is not significantly different from the proportions for the sample as a whole.

Regular v. *occasional takers.* Ten of the thirty-seven males (27 per cent) and five (23 per cent) of the females were regular drug-takers. The females are therefore just as likely to be regular takers as the males.

Position in school. Fourteen males (37 per cent) and six females (27 per cent) said they were in the top ten positions in their form. There was no significant difference between the two groups.

Trouble with the police. Twenty-two of the males (59 per cent) had been in trouble with the police as compared with twelve (55 per cent) of the females. The females were therefore just as likely to be delinquent as the males.

Spare time activities. As might be expected significantly more males (43 per cent) than females (9 per cent) played sport for their school or club. There were no significant differences between the numbers of boys and girls who went out with girls or with boys, or with both boys and girls. Similarly there was no significant difference between the number of boys who went out with a girl friend (24 per cent) and the number of girls who went out with a boy friend (32 per cent). As there was no significant difference in the ages of the two groups, 41 per cent of the females and 54 per cent of the males being fifteen or younger, the implication is that for this group the boys were as heterosexually advanced as the females in terms of mixed peer groups. A final significant difference as regards spare time activities was that 82 per cent of the girls went dancing at least once a week compared to only 35 per cent of the males.

Smoking. This similarity between the two groups is reinforced by the figures for smoking where 81 per cent of the males and 77 per cent of the females smoked. Nor was there any difference as regards the quantity of cigarettes consumed: 73 per cent of the males to 59 per cent of the females smoked more than 20 cigarettes a week (no significant difference).

Personal problems. There were no differences between the two groups in terms of who they referred to when they had a personal problem.

From these findings it must be concluded that as far as drug-taking goes there are virtually no differences between the male and female takers at school level, at least in terms of this study. The females are just as likely to take drugs as the males, are just as likely to be regular takers and to have been in trouble with the police.

SUMMARY OF THE MAIN FINDINGS

1 Questionnaires were given to 1093 subjects from the four different areas. The majority of the subjects came from the area with the highest reported incidence of drug-taking. As regards the distribution of the subjects on the variables of age, social class, sex and trouble with the police there was comparatively little difference between the four areas. Fewer than half the subjects who completed questionnaires were school leavers.

2 Fifty-nine of the subjects, 5·39 per cent of the sample, had taken drugs. Of these, 75 per cent were occasional users only. For various reasons, the figure of 5·39 per cent is felt to be an under-estimation of the true figure for drug-taking in the schools studied. Of the 59 drug users, 35 had taken one drug only, 15 had taken two drugs, 8 had taken three drugs and one had tried four different drugs. Subjects also reported a wide range of effects on their first drug experience.

3 The drug-takers were representative of the sample as a whole in terms of the ratio of male to female drug users. They tended to be found among the older subjects and to come from white-collar backgrounds. They were also more likely to be school leavers.

4 Compared to matched controls, drug-takers were less likely to refer to their parents with a personal problem, they felt less

close to their mother and felt that their parents had been more lenient with them. They also felt that they did worse at school and reported that they had been in trouble with the police more frequently than the controls did.

5 The leisure activities of the drug-takers, when compared to that of the controls, was more typical of the behaviour of an older age group. For example they went to pubs, dancing and to Soho. Drug-takers also had more money to spend and tended to spend it on clothes, cigarettes, drinks and drugs. They smoked and drank more than did the controls and tended to mix in peer groups whose members also smoked, drank and took drugs. The drug-takers spent more time in mixed peer group company than did the controls and were less nervous about peer group relationships.

6 Drug-takers did not differ markedly from controls in terms of their attitudes to life though they did tend to say they were more impulsive and had less respect for property. In comparison to the controls, drug-takers had markedly more favourable attitudes to drugs and more knowledge about drugs. In the sample as a whole few people knew very much about drugs, though on the other hand there was comparatively little inaccurate knowledge about drugs.

7 On factoring the three perceptual scales, four factors were identified. These were factors of conventionality, weakness, obedience and heterosexual appeal. On the factor of conventionality both drug-takers and controls perceived themselves to be more unconventional than their ideal selves and perceived people who took drugs as more unconventional than themselves. On the second factor, weakness, both groups perceived people who take drugs as being tougher than their ideal selves but while the controls perceived no difference between their self image and that of their ideal self, the drug-takers perceived no difference between their own image and that of the person who takes drugs. On the third factor of obedience, both groups perceived people who take drugs to be more disobedient than themselves and while the drug-takers perceived themselves to be more disobedient than their ideal selves, the controls saw no difference between themselves and their ideal self. Finally, on factor four the controls perceived no difference as regards heterosexual appeal between themselves, their ideal selves and people who take drugs. The drug-takers, however, perceived people who take drugs as having more heterosexual appeal than themselves though they saw no difference between themselves and their ideal self.

8 By their comments at the end of the questionnaire subjects indicated that on the whole they did not realise the true purpose of the questionnaire.

9 There were few differences between the regular and occasional drug users, the delinquent and non-delinquent drug users and between the male and female drug users. The few differences that existed indicated that the regular user was one step beyond the occasional user in the degree of his pattern of behaviour.

9 Discussion and recommendations

DISCUSSION

The results indicate that drug-takers at school level can be differentiated from non-drug-takers on a number of variables. These variables can be grouped meaningfully into three patterns. In the first the drug-takers, when compared to the controls, were less nervous about peer group relationships, spent more time with peer groups and more time in mixed company. Also the drug-takers, in comparison to the controls, saw people who take drugs as having more heterosexual appeal than they perceived themselves to have. They spent less time with their parents, referred to them less often when they had a personal problem, felt they were more lenient and that they, when compared to the controls, were further removed from their mother. In their leisure time, when compared to the controls, the drug-takers more frequently visited pubs, coffee bars, dance halls, etc. They also had more money to spend and tended to spend it on cigarettes, drinks and drugs while the controls were more likely to save their money. The drug-takers drank and smoked more than the controls did and mixed in peer groups whose members also tended to drink, smoke and take drugs. In comparison fewer controls smoked and drank and similarly fewer members of their peer groups smoked and drank. The pattern that emerges from all these differences is that drug-takers tend to live a life more typical of an older teenage group.

In the second pattern that emerges the drug-takers, in comparison to the controls, saw themselves as more disobedient, had less respect for property and were more impulsive. They had been in trouble with the police more often and knew more people who had been in trouble with the police. Similarly, on the concept of toughness, drug-takers perceived no difference between their perception of people who take drugs and their own self image. In comparison the controls perceived the people who take drugs to be tougher than they perceived themselves to be. Drug-takers also said that they did significantly worse at school. This pattern could be said to represent a delinquent outlook on life by the drug-taker.

In the third group of differences, the drug-takers knew more people who had taken drugs, they had more favourable attitudes to drugs and had more knowledge about them when compared to the controls. This pattern simply indicates that drug-takers know more about drugs than non-drug-takers do.

Four main questions can be asked about this data: (1) Why did only these three patterns emerge? (2) What is the interrelationship between these three patterns? (3) How do these patterns tie in with previous findings? (4) What are the implications of these patterns?

The first question is important because the hypotheses had predicted on the basis of previous findings in the fields of drug-taking and deviance that a fourth pattern would have emerged. This would have involved difference between the drug-takers and the controls in terms of family structure, personality and socio-economic class; that is the deprived environmental background pattern. No differences in the actual survey were found on family background factors nor on personality factors and even though there were differences in social class concentration between the drug-takers and the controls, there were drug-takers in the sample from all the social classes. One reason for this pattern not emerging is that the evidence on which the hypotheses were based came mainly from American sources and were based on research into heroin addicts, not occasional drug users. In fact studies of occasional drug users had indicated that they were not necessarily disturbed individuals. Another reason might be that the whole problem of deprivation was not gone into in sufficient complexity in the questionnaire.

The second question asks in what way are the patterns related. Is the fact that drug-takers are more delinquent related to the fact that they adopt an older style of behaviour? It might be that these are two different patterns of drug use among school children. The number of drug-takers in this sample does not permit this sort of analysis of the data. Yet it is also possible to see a relationship between these two patterns. If the drug-takers adopt a life style more typical of an older age group they will tend to be among the youngest present at pubs, coffee bars, discotheques, etc. If the police raid the places these people, because of their youth, are likely to be picked up. However, this is conjecture, as to some extent is the solution of the problem of whether the drug-takers had more knowledge about drugs before they started using them, say for example, because they were mixing with an older age group, or whether the knowledge only came with drug use. In fact trying to impose a temporal sequence upon the ordering of the patterns and of the differences within them is very difficult within a cross-sectional framework. Without such an ordering it becomes impossible to talk in terms of causality. However, all three patterns tend to indicate that factors in the subjects' immediate environment play a very important part in determining drug use.

The third question asks how these patterns fit in with previous findings. It has already been seen that in contradiction to what was expected, environmental background did not play an important part. In taking the first pattern the most striking thing about it is its similarity to the findings of the Government Social Survey's study (95) of cigarette smoking. Similarly the fact that drug-takers were further removed from their parents and spent more time with their peers indicates that peer groups were functioning also as reference groups for the drug-takers. This implies that the group a person belongs to influences the behaviour he adopts, provided this group functions as his reference group. A different interpretation of these findings is possible. That is that the person started taking drugs or smoking or drinking alcohol before joining a deviant group and it was only through indulging in this behaviour that they gained entrance to the group. Also, of course, reference group pressure, whatever the case, was only one influence in determining whether someone took drugs. This is shown by the fact that some drug-takers were members of groups which did not take drugs and that some non-users were members of drug-taking groups. Earlier studies had found that drug-taking was related to the availability of drugs. This study would tend to support this observation. First, there were a significantly greater proportion of drug-takers in the schools in the very high area than in the medium area, and secondly, the drug-takers tended to frequent the places where drugs would most likely be found.

Previous findings had indicated that as regards delinquency, the drug-taking situation was that some delinquents were drug-takers and that some drug-takers were delinquent in ways other than drug-taking. This is the pattern that emerged here. Many, but not all, of the drug-takers had been in trouble with the police, as had some of the non-drug-takers. Perhaps this section should also mention the relationship between the images obtained on the perceptual scales in this study and those obtained by

McKennell and Bynner. In fact the two analyses did not prove to be directly comparable. Whereas McKennell and Bynner (153:30) had found only three factors with a latent root >1, this study found six, and whereas McKennell and Bynner had one large general factor which accounted for much of the variance this did not emerge in this case. In fact the only directly similar factor identified as such in both bases was that of toughness.

As regards the pattern of knowledge about drugs, there had been little previous research on soft drug users, though what was expected was that the more favourable the attitudes one held towards drugs the more likely one was to take drugs, and if one took drugs the more knowledge one would have about them. While these two expectations were supported by the results it is difficult to know to what extent the attitudes and the knowledge existed before the drug use and to what extent they were a result of it. The fact that regular drug users had more favourable attitudes than the occasional users indicates that attitudes to drugs are related to the degree of drug use. One point that the literature had made was that while some people knew the dangers of heroin before they started using it, others were not aware of its dangers. The figures show that in fact there was a general lack of knowledge about drugs as in thirty-six out of the forty-seven drug knowledge items over 40 per cent of the total sample did not know what the right answer was.

The fourth question considers what implications these patterns of behaviour have. There appear to be three important areas to consider in this regard. First, what is the implication as regards the reasons for taking drugs? The second area concerns what is to be done with the problem, and the third concerns the area of education.

One of the main interests in the first area is whether the findings can help to explain why people take drugs while at school. There are two levels at which this problem can be answered. The first and more general one is whether there are any general factors which account for why people take drugs, for example a psychopathic personality. At this level, as has already been pointed out, it is difficult for a cross-cultural study to talk in terms of causality. What one can say is that it is unlikely that there is any one reason which explains why some people take drugs. Any such reason would have to be able to account for all the differences found between drug-takers and non-drug-takers. But as the results revealed there were many differences between the drug-takers and the controls. That is, drug-taking is multicausal and is related to other teenage problems like delinquency and smoking. It follows from this that there are no simple answers to the problem of drug-taking. What is likely in fact is that all of these differences in some way play a part in determining who takes drugs and the part each factor plays changes from individual to individual. At a more specific level one can always ask why did someone take a drug in this particular circumstance and perhaps not in another. Again there is no one answer, for example the nine subjects who said why they first took a drug gave between them eight different reasons.

The second part of this question concerns implications for treating drug-taking as a problem. The results of this survey suggest that at the most, only 10 per cent of the school population have tried drugs and that of these only a quarter or less take them with any degree of regularity. This means that without any, or with only a minimum, of education on the topic three-quarters of those who try drugs either stop using them after the first experience or continue taking them only on a sporadic basis. The indication is that drug-taking at this level is mainly an experimentation, a passing through stage. In fact, as the next section will discuss, to treat drug-taking as a major problem when it isn't one, is likely to make it into one. While drug-taking exists in the society at large there will always be a minority of those at school who experiment with them. As drug-taking appears to be on the increase in America despite punitive measures against it, it might well prove to be the case that drug-taking in the immediate future will continue to increase whatever course of action is taken by the authorities. If this is so the problem becomes one of educating people to be able to differentiate between drugs which are potentially damaging and those which are comparatively safe. This is probably a longer term consideration. In the short term the only serious problem concerns the minority of subjects who might not at this stage be users but who will later be tempted to try hard drugs. Till a longitudinal study has been able to isolate these individuals it might well be best to treat drug-taking at school level as a passing experimental stage where no major action is needed.

The third part of this question concerns the implications of these findings for an educational policy. The next section will discuss the feasibility of an educational programme in schools at this time. The first point is that the answers of the total sample to the drug knowledge items indicate most school children have comparatively little knowledge about drug-taking. However, they also have very little incorrect knowledge about drugs. This means that any educational policy would have the easier task of filling gaps in education rather than the more difficult one of having to change incorrect beliefs. Finally the answers of the total sample on the individual drug attitude items indicates that generally speaking non-drug users have unfavourable opinions about most aspects of drug use and that the main problem of an educational campaign, which was aimed at prevention, would be to alter the favourable beliefs about drugs that are held by those who take them.

RECOMMENDATIONS

One of the aims of this study was to look into the feasibility of an educational policy upon drugs. The first part of this section discusses this point before wondering briefly just why everyone sees drugs as a problem. The second part considers the implications of this study for further research into drug-taking.

Education

The first point that needs to be reinforced is that drug-taking at school level is not a widespread problem. It was estimated that at the most 10 per cent of the school population might have tried drugs of whom only a quarter could in any sense be considered regular users.

The second point is that there is no guarantee that any sort of preventive education campaign among school children would be successful. If one considers the related field of smoking, 'a recent report carried out for the Ministry of Health points out that school smoking policy and health education have had little effect upon young people' (68:140). In fact, as the previous section showed, the policy of non-education has been quite successful in so far as only a quarter of those who try drugs end by taking them with any degree of regularity. The difficulty of education is that those who do become regular users, and who are the ones that any policy would be aimed at, might well be those who are most resistant to any form of education. In trying to reach them there is a danger that any campaign would have the reverse effect to that intended, and in fact create a larger problem. This is first, because as drugs are only taken by a minority of school children, any campaign is likely to bring the whole topic to the awareness of many children who would otherwise never have become concerned about it. A second reason is that if a large-scale educational campaign is mounted this serves to elevate drugs to the equivalent status of cigarette smoking as a problem. Children might well then argue that if drug-taking is so widespread, it cannot be as harmful as the authorities make out, and also that they ought to try drugs if they don't want to be left out of it.

One of the reasons for the probable lack of success of any such campaign is that knowledge and attitudes, which are two of the aspects of drug-taking that can best be handled in the school-room, are not necessarily the most important factors in determining drug use among school children. Other factors, like availability, peer group pressure and rebellion which also play a part in determining drug use, are not as easily handled within the school system. The same point has been made about cigarette smoking.

But even if one decided to have a campaign on drugs, there are a number of problems one would have to solve. First, what would the message of any campaign be? Any message must be truthful and cannot exaggerate the dangers because if 10 per cent of the school population have some knowledge about drugs they will know that the occasional use of drugs like cannabis is not inherently harmful. If the message is truthful then it must point out that while drugs like methylamphetamine and heroin if taken with any degree of frequency are potentially very dangerous, the occasional use of most drugs, particularly cannabis, is not. Similarly the message should not be one of horror. The psychological literature on attitude change (some examples of this are given in Part 3 of the bibliography) indicates that attitude change is a complex phenomena and that any attempt to change attitudes by fear alone is unlikely to succeed.

A second problem involves deciding who should communicate the message. Should one have an ex-addict or does this merely glamourise the whole business? Should it be the police—but they are hardly likely to be seen as being neutral in this situation by the young people they are trying to reach? A third problem concerns the aim of any educational programme. Is one attempting to achieve the total abolition of drug use? If so, any programme is unlikely to be successful because for some the very illegality of the drugs will be a reason for taking them.

For all these reasons I would like to argue that until more research has been carried out any educational campaign in schools raises more problems than it is likely to solve. However, I do believe that a case can be made out for education aimed at reaching those who already take drugs. The suggestion is that education should be carried out in the areas where drugs are taken, such as Soho. The advantage of this is that it would also reach many of the schoolchildren who are already regular drug users without the risk of 'contaminating' the rest. Such a campaign should be carried out through the agencies of the detached social worker,[1] underground newspapers, etc., i.e., through any source which these people are likely to pay attention to. Any such campaign must be realistic. It should concentrate upon teaching young people about the dangers of drugs like methedrine and heroin. Such a campaign should not and could not be expected to recommend the complete abstension from drug use while drugs like cannabis remain part of the scene. All large cities have their dance halls and their coffee bars where drugs are pushed and where the detached social worker can come into contact with the regular drug users. It is these, the regular users, that any campaign should aim at reaching.

If any campaign were to be carried out with school children, the most appropriate way to introduce it would seem to be as part of a general discussion series with school leavers on problems in the community. It could well be argued that there is a need for a school course at all levels which is solely concerned with problems of adjustment to a rapidly changing environment. Besides dealing with drug-taking it could also tackle the increasing problem of venereal disease, and could well be wide enough to cover the whole field of sex education. Such a course could also include the possible problem of coping with leisure in a highly automated society and other modern difficulties such as the bias in news reporting which results from the telecommunication age. Whatever the scope of such a course it would require specially trained teachers. One cannot expect a teacher trained in English to be successful in taking a discussion on the ethics and dangers of fixing heroin.

Finally, it is possible to look at the whole problem from a different perspective and ask the question of why society expends so much energy and indignation on condemning the taking of drugs.

---

[1] Detached social workers appear to have come about through a curious process. Originally the aim of social work was to help the less fortunate in society. To do this successfully it was of course necessary for the social worker to be able to establish rapport with those whom he wished to assist. However, as social work grew and grew, it became, as all such aspiring professions do, more 'respectable' and bureacratic. Soon social workers were required to have degrees and diplomas and were expected to work a 9–5 day. Then after a while it became apparent that there were whole groups of people in society who were in need of help but who didn't take to respectable people nor live 9–5 lives. Thus a whole new breed of social worker was formed—people normally without degrees who have the ability to get on with deviants and who are prepared to work all hours of day and night.

It condones with only minor protest the taking of nicotine and alcohol. It accepts with virtually no protest the greater social costs that accrue from heart attacks and from road accidents involving pedestrians. So why are drugs considered such a problem? It has in fact been contended that the drug problem is, why are drugs perceived as a problem? One possible answer to this that I would like to suggest is that the only way the mass of society knows it is being moral is by having an outgroup who are classified as being immoral. Various groups in the past seem to have served this function as an outgroup—adulterers, homosexuals, indulgers in premarital sexuality, etc. However, in time society comes to realise that many of its own members in fact indulge in these practices and it is therefore no longer able to condemn that particular group without risking dissension within its own ranks. It can be argued that drug-takers and militant students are the two present outgroups which serve the function of giving society a moral standard and also of unifying it against them. This is, however, an untested hypothesis which would require more than circumstantial evidence before it could be accepted.

Recommendations for further research

This section proposes first, to look at where further research is required in the field of drugs, and secondly, at some of the problems that this study found in working with school children and possible steps by which they can be remedied in the future.

1 The present study has helped to identify the occasional drug-taker who is still at school. What is required as a direct follow-up of this study is one which will discover which occasional takers become regular drug users and which will either remain occasional users or give up taking them altogether. It is the former group which present the biggest potential social problem and amongst them the important differentiation to be made is between those who remain on soft drugs and the minority who escalate to hard drug use.

The ideal design to study this is a longitudinal one. It would be most effective if it took a sample of school children in their final year at school and followed them up for a number of years. Diagrammatically this would mean:

Though this picture is grossly oversimplified it does indicate the sort of comparisons that can be made, i.e. between those who become regular drug users and those who become occasional drug users: between those who start off as non-drug users and become regular drug users and those who start off as occasional drug users and then stop, etc. This is one of the most important pieces of research which has to be done in this field.

2 A second area where research is needed is in the field of drug education. There is a need here to find out:

(a) who should deliver the message about drugs to which sort of audience? Should it be someone who is actually taking drugs, an ex-addict, a police officer, a social scientist?

(b) the precise content of the message. Should it be emotional or factual in tone? At what level should it be pitched? Should it only concentrate on one drug or should it cover the whole field?

(c) the most appropriate situation in which to communicate the mesage.

(d) how effective the media about drugs in present use are. A number of schools and educational institutions show films on drugs or have guest speakers who address themselves either to the pupils or their parents. Yet to the best of my knowledge no one is measuring how effective these attempts at education are.

There is at the moment a belief that films are the most appropriate medium by which the population's attitudes will be changed. A number of these films are in the process of being produced yet there is comparatively little evidence that they will be effective. The need for research is therefore important.

The above list is by no means comprehensive. However, it is unlikely that unless the merits of all the above choices are carefully weighed before any media is prepared, any communication on drugs will probably be ineffective.

3 There are two other areas where research is needed, though they themselves are not directly related to this particular study. The first of these is in finding out more about the subjects who take drugs but who never appear before a court or other institution. This is important for a number of reasons. First, till more is known about these subjects one will not know how unrepresentative samples are that are drawn from institutionalised drug-takers. Secondly, drug effects are dependent to some extent upon the situation in which they are taken. For this reason experimental studies of the effects of various drugs need to be supplemented by participant observation studies of drug use in different subcultures. Thirdly, it is impossible to know how big a general

problem drug-taking is till one has some accurate idea of how many drug-takers are at present 'unknown'.

4 The other obvious area where research is needed concerns the effectiveness of different methods of treatment of addicts. One cannot hope to get rid of the heroin problem till some way is found of keeping addicts off the drug once they have been withdrawn from it. Attempts to reduce the amount of heroin in circulation are a part of the step, but the other and more difficult is to give withdrawn addicts a life style which they can live with without needing to turn to drugs. There are many different forms of treatment now in operation: the use of methadone, hostel schemes, Synanon, etc. They all seem to work to a limited extent with a particular type of addict. What is needed is a project which will find out what type of addict responds best to what type of treatment.

5 A final point on research is that there are a number of organisations working in the drug field. Yet there is limited contact between them and in some cases there is mistrust. Yet if a way could be found to standardise the information that all of these organisations collect about the drug-takers they see, there would be a wealth of information about the numbers of drug-takers, types of drugs used, etc. There is a need for a research body, not to go and collect new data, but to standardise and analyse the data that is already in existence.

PROBLEMS OF WORKING WITH SCHOOL CHILDREN

(a) Sampling. In any work involving drugs and school children there is likely to be a problem of random sampling. It is obviously easy to draw up a random sample of schools and/or school children in a district but with present societal attitudes on the subject it is unlikely that all those chosen will cooperate. The evidence for this comes from the attempt to draw a random sample in the second sample in this study. If it is not possible to obtain a random sample it seems best to abandon the principle of randomness altogether. This is because if in a random sample some schools cooperate while others do not, one does not know how these schools differ from those who do not cooperate. An alternative principle, and the one used here, is to rate all the schools on a criterion, such as the likelihood of their having drug-takers, and select them on this basis. Then, even if some of the chosen schools cooperate while others do not, one still has some basis on which to compare them. The advantage of this particular criterion as a substitute for randomness is that one can conclude that the problem is unlikely to be any worse in other schools in the district if one has selected those most likely to have drug-takers.

A second point on sampling concerns the criteria of representativeness used when stratifying a sample. Normally with schools one tries to make sure that schools in an area are representative of type, whether grammar, comprehensive, public, etc., and sex. However, few, if any, studies ever appear to have controlled for the 'interaction between the headmaster and the school'. This was a point which impressed the research team in the schools in which they entered. For example it was possible to visit schools in the same area of the same type and sex, yet where the 'atmosphere' would be quite different. This point is illustrated by the fact that in one school after the headmaster had introduced the team and left there was perfect quietness and complete cooperation, yet in a similar type of school, immediately the headmaster left, talking, fidgeting, attempts to cheat, etc., occurred. The impression on the research team was that this relationship between the headmaster and the rest of the school might be as important to consider as the type of school when drawing up a sample.

(b) *Truancy.* Any future study will have to come to grips with the already mentioned problem of truancy. One way to do this would be to leave questionnaires behind to be filled in under supervision when the subjects returned to school.

(c) *Confidentiality.* In any longitudinal study subjects will have to be identified by name. This can be done either secretly or openly. If done openly it might well be that some subjects might be more tempted to lie to a questionnaire. If done secretly, on the other hand, some subjects, if they find out later, might not be willing to cooperate at a later stage of the survey.

(d) *Validity.* If a project is large enough to enable the use of interviews rather than questionnaires, this naturally gives more opportunity for the verification of subjects' answers. If a questionnaire is going to be used for the first stage of a longitudinal study then, as the identity of the subjects will be known, interviews should be carried out with a random sample of the respondents.

(e) *Administrative problems.* There were a number of small administrative difficulties with schools that a future survey might be able to avoid. The first of these is to make sure that subjects who finish first can leave the test room, otherwise with nothing to do they tend to disturb those still finishing. Secondly, the ideal arrangement is where the subjects are seated in examination conditions. This is difficult to arrange as in most classrooms pupils sit two to a desk, and many schools do not have large enough halls to accommodate all school leavers at one to a desk. It might well be preferable in this case to have two testing sessions.

The third and final administrative point is that the larger the group within the school tested at one sitting, the greater the need to have a teacher present to maintain discipline. It is also important to have a talk to this teacher beforehand and warn him of the dangers of disturbing subjects by peering over their shoulders, etc.

In conclusion, this section has argued that there is a need for a limited educational programme and finally has pointed to a need for more research into drug-taking.

APPENDIX A

Drugs used and frequency of usage

ONE-DRUG USERS: N = 35

11 subjects said they had taken pep pills once only

6 subjects said they had taken hashish once only

2 subjects said they had now stopped using pep pills

4 subjects said they had taken pep pills less than 5 times

3 subjects said they had taken hashish less than 5 times

1 subject said he had taken LSD less than 5 times

3 subjects said they took pep pills sometimes at weekends or parties

2 subjects said they took hashish sometimes at weekends or parties

1 subject said he took an unnamed drug at weekends or parties

1 subject said he took hashish 1–5 times weekly

1 subject said he had taken pep pills less than 5 times at weekends or parties.

TWO-DRUG USERS: N = 15

(a) PEP pills/hashish: N = 8

SUBJECT NO.

1 pep pills—less than 5 times—now stopped taking them
hashish—taken once—now stopped taking it.

2 pep pills—less than 5 times—now stopped taking them
hashish—sometimes at weekends or parties.

3 pep pills—once only at a weekend or party
hashish—once only at weekend or party.

4 pep pills—once only
hashish—once only.

5 pep pills—less than five times
hashish—once only.

6 pep pills—now stopped taking them
hashish once only.

7 pep pills—sometimes at weekends or parties
hashish—now stopped taking it.

8 pep pills—once only
hashish—less than five times.

(b) PEP pills/LSD: N = 3

SUBJECT NO.

1 pep pills—sometimes at weekends or parties
LSD—once only.

2 pep pills—once only—now stopped taking them
LSD—once only—now stopped taking it.

3 pep pills—less than five times
LSD—once only.

(c) Hashish/LSD: N = 2

SUBJECT NO.

1 hashish—now stopped taking it
LSD—once only.

2 hashish—sometimes at weekends or parties
LSD—once only.

(d) Hashish/Heroin: N = 2

SUBJECT NO.

1 hashish—once only—now stopped taking it
Heroin—sometimes take this at weekends or parties.

2 hashish—now stopped taking it
Heroin—now stopped taking them.

THREE-DRUG USERS: N = 8

(a) PEP pills/LSD/hashish: N = 5

SUBJECT NO.

1 pep pills—once only
  LSD—less than five times
  hashish—now stopped taking this drug.

2 pep pills—once only
  LSD—less than five times
  hashish—1-5 times weekly—now stopped taking this drug.

3 pep pills—once only—now stopped taking this drug
  LSD—once only
  hashish—sometimes at weekends or parties.

4 pep pills—once only
  LSD—less than five times
  hashish—now stopped taking this drug.

5 pep pills—once only—at weekend or party—now stopped
  LSD—less than five times
  hashish—once only—now stopped taking this drug.

(b) PEP pills/hashish/heroin: N = 2

1 pep pills—less than five times
  hashish—less than five times—sometimes at weekends or
  parties
  heroin—sometimes at weekends or parties—now stopped.

2 pep pills—less than five times
  hashish—sometimes at weekends or parties
  heroin—now stopped taking this drug.

(c) PEP pills/hashish/others: N = 1

1 pep pills—now stopped taking this drug
  hashish—now stopped taking this drug
  other—now stopped taking this drug.

FOUR-DRUG USER: N = 1

PEP pills/hashish/LSD/heroin

1 pep pills—less than five times—now stopped taking
  hashish—less than five times—now stopped taking
  LSD—sometimes at weekends or parties
  heroin—once only.

APPENDIX B

Additional Tables

1 DRUG-TAKERS BY SCHOOL

School	Number of drug-takers in the school	Drug-takers as % of school population tested
1	4	3·7
2	19	4·4
3	2	2·9
4	3	4·1
5	0	0
6	6	14·6
7	9	10·0
8	10	8·0
9	6	7·1

2 SCHOOL BY SEX OF SUBJECTS

School	Non-drug-takers Male	Female	Drug-takers Male	Female
1	49	55	2	2
2	233	182	10	9
3	33	32	2	—
4	38	33	1	2
5	36	34	—	—
6	35	—	6	—
7	—	81	—	9
8	115	—	10	—
9	78	—	6	—
Total N =	617	417	37	22
% =	59·8	41·2	62·8	37·2

3 SCHOOL BY TROUBLE WITH THE POLICE

School	Non-drug-takers (figures in percentages)		Drug-takers (figures in numbers)	
	Have been in trouble	Not been in trouble	Have been in trouble	Not been in trouble
1	24·5	75·5	4	
2	14·9	84·1	11	8
3	15·4	84·6	1	1
4	21·1	79·0	2	1
5	14·1	84·5	—	—
6	17·4	82·6	2	4
7	3·7	96·2	3	6
8	19·7	80·7	7	3
9	19·0	78·5	4	2
Total N =	168	857	34	25
% =	16·3	83·2	57·6	42·4
No answer =	6.			

4 SCHOOL BY SOCIAL CLASS (Hall-Jones scale)

School	Non drug users (figures in percentages)						Drug users (figures in raw scores)				
	1/2	3/4	5a	5b	6/7	N/A	1/2	3/4	5a	5b	6/7
1	0·9	10·5	8·5	41·3	20·2	14·2	0	1	1	1	
2	12·0	24·2	6·8	35·9	8·8	11·7	3	9	1	4	2
3	4·6	21·5	9·2	44·6	16·9	3·1		2			
4		7·0	11·3	47·9	18·3	15·5			1	1	1
5		15·5	4·2	40·8	25·3	14·1					
6	8·6	17·2	17·1	34·3	17·2	5·7	2	1			
7	32·6	16·3	11·3	32·5		7·5	1	3	1	4	
8	14·9	26·3	8·8	36·0	4·4	9·6	1	3	1	4	
9	20·3	26·3	8·9	27·8	6·3	10·1	3	2	1		
Total											
N =	116	212	86	383	115		10	21	6	14	3
% =	11·2	20·6	8·3	37·1	11·1	11·0	16·9	35·6	10·2	23·7	5·1

APPENDIX C

Reliability and validity

The two terms are described by Oppenheim (224:73) as follows: 'Reliability refers to consistency, to obtaining the same results again. Validity tells us whether the question or item really measures what it is supposed to measure.'

There are different ways of assessing the validity of questionnaires. They include construct validity in which 'validity is inferred from . . . a predicted network of relationships'. (Oppenheim 224:75). Another method is to compare the findings with those from another survey in the same field. No such data was available in this case. A final method is that of criterion validity where 'a criterion is an independent measure of the same variable, to which the results of our test or questionnaire can be compared'. (Oppenheim: 224:75). In some of the questionnaires, because of the problem of confidentiality and the absence of appropriate and easily obtainable criterion groups, validity is difficult to ascertain.

There are two basic types of reliability. There is reliability over time (test/retest reliability) and there is consistency within a particular questionnaire. It was not possible in any of the questionnaires to measure reliability over time. This would have meant repeating the questionnaires on the same sample after an interval of a month or so. This was impossible to do because final examinations were approaching and the schools would have been unlikely to cooperate. An attempt was made to give the attitude-to-drugs scale to subjects before and after a youth club conference on drugs but administrative arrangements fell through. Therefore the only reliability measures that one could use were concerned with the internal consistency of the questionnaires. On factual questions it is important to make sure that all related answers are consistent; otherwise one must doubt the validity of the answers. As regards attitudinal items the argument is that the more homogeneous the items the more sure one can be that the underlying attitude is common to all items in the scale.

QUESTIONNAIRE A

The main problem in this questionnaire is whether questions 26 and 27 really show which subjects take drugs and which subjects do not. The most appropriate type of validity test to have used would have been some form of criterion validity. One such suggested criterion was the urine test as used for example by Scott and Willcox (180). However, though this test might be appropriate for small groups in a remand home it was not applicable in this case for a number of reasons. These are:

1 The urine test can at the moment only detect traces of amphetamines but not of cannabis and LSD. Therefore subjects who took drugs other than amphetamines would not be detected.

2 The test only shows effects of drugs taken within the previous thirty-six hours and would therefore only be expected to pick up regular drug users, or at least those who took them every weekend provided the test was given first thing Monday morning. As the pilot study had indicated that the majority of the drug-takers were likely to be occasional users the test did not seem appropriate.

3 To be an accurate validation measure there would have had to be a matching of urine samples and questionnaire responses. This would only have given a meaningful result in this survey if there had been more positive urine tests than the numbers admitting taking drugs on the questionnaires. If the number of positive urine samples had been equal to or fewer than the questionnaire responses admitting taking drugs, then one would have learnt nothing about the validity of the questionnaires.

4 If matching was necessary this raises problems of confidentiality.

5 If the urine test is given first then there is a danger that the subjects might realise the purpose of the test and subsequently deny drug-taking experiences in the questionnaire. If the urine test is not given immediately after the questionnaire then the

drug-taking pattern of subjects might have changed in the interval.

For these reasons the urine test seemed to be an inappropriate criterion.

The only other type of feasible criterion measure would have been to find some independent way of knowing which of the school children had taken drugs. A possible way of doing this would have been for someone else to have carried out follow-up interviews of some of the subjects without being told first which were drug-takers and which were not. However, because of the problems of confidentiality and probable difficulties in cooperation with local education authorities, this could not be done.

The fallback position adopted in this survey was getting the subjects themselves to estimate the number of drug-takers within a school. Though this obviously cannot be a precise measure, it was hoped to obtain a range within which the number of drug-takers found in the survey ought to fall. However, as the section in Chapter 8 showed that even though in the three schools within which this was carried out the majority of the non-drug-takers estimated accurately that there were less than twenty-five drug takers within each school, the estimates of the drug-takers themselves ranged from less than six to over a hundred.

The same problems of validity apply to nearly all the factual questions in Questionnaire A. However, to consider the problem from the other point of view, there are few indications that subjects did not tell the truth. In fact not one single set of questionnaires, excluding the three discarded because of the subject's lack of English, was completed in such a way that it had to be discounted, and over 95 per cent of the comments about the questionnaire indicated that the subjects had taken it seriously. Also all the steps taken to preserve the anonymity of the questionnaire responses would serve to encourage subjects to tell the truth, and studies, for example that of Ball (6), have shown that under the right conditions deviants are prepared to be truthful about their behaviour.

The problem of the consistency of the answers to drug-taking questions has already been discussed in the beginning of Chapter 8. On none of the other topics covered in this questionnaire was there a sufficient range of questions for problems of internal consistency to apply.

QUESTIONNAIRE B

To test the reliability of this questionnaire a component analysis was carried out on the answers of the fifty-nine drug-takers and the fifty-nine controls. If the test was reliable then one would expect that there would be inter-item consistency: that is that the items measuring the same thing should be correlated. One would therefore expect if the scale was measuring six variables that six groupings of items should appear. In fact the first five first order factors, latent root >1, were very similar to the predicted groupings of items measuring closeness to mother, parental leniency, poor group relations, parental control and closeness to father. The only set of items which did not appear to be correlated were those measuring ego strength. Therefore the lack of internal consistency of this set of items casts doubt on their validity as a measure of ego strength. In the case of the other five sets of items it was impossible to check their validity as there were no readily available criterion groups.

QUESTIONNAIRE F

As the final version of this questionnaire is very similar to that used in the pilot study it is possible to treat the heroin addicts to whom the pilot version was given as a criterion group. If the questionnaire was measuring drug knowledge then one would expect that addicts would score higher than the drug users in the pilot sample. This in fact proved to be the case when Mann-Whitney U Test was applied to the scores of the two groups.

It was possible to test the internal consistency of the answers to this questionnaire as questions 19 and 37 were in fact the same question asked in different ways:

Q.19: Marijuana and hashish are different preparations from the same plant.
Q.37: Marijuana is made from the same plant as hashish.

If the questionnaire was reliable one would expect that there would be no difference in the percentage of subjects who answered question 19 correctly and the percentage who answered question 37 correctly. When the answers of the total sample ($N=1089$)

were analysed this in fact proved to be the case as 20·8 per cent of the sample answered question 19 correctly and 19·7 per cent answered question 37 correctly.

QUESTIONNAIRE G and C

In neither of these questionnaires was there a readily available criterion group to test their validity and similarly it was impossible to carry out a test/retest reliability. As Questionnaire G was meant to be a unidimensional scale measuring attitudes to drugs it was possible to carry out a split-half reliability test on it. Scores on the eight even items were compared to scores on the nine odd items in the scale. The correlation test was the Spearman rank correlation coefficient and the finding was that $r_s = 0.565$, which is significantly different from zero.

QUESTIONNAIRES D, E and H

For these three questionnaires there was no appropriate validity measure readily available nor was it possible to carry out a test/retest reliability check on them.

APPENDIX D

The Questionnaire

KINDS OF QUESTIONS

1 On how many evenings a week do you watch television?

one ....   three ....

two ....   four ......✓...............

2 Below are a number of statements about how young people feel about things. Each statement is paired with another. You have to choose which of the two statements in each pair you agree with most and then place a tick beside it.

Cricket is an interesting sport ....

or

Cricket is a boring sport ....

3 Choose the words which best describe the kind of person you are. Each word will be paired with another like this.

nice   [✓]   [   ]   [   ]   nasty

	Strongly agree	*Agree*	*Uncertain*	*Disagree*	*Strongly disagree*
4 Footballers are great people		✓			

	True	*False*	*Don't know*
5 The ark was built by Noah			

6 Do you ever do the pools or have a bet?

    (*tick one*)   yes ....

                                                  no ....

If yes to question 6
How many times a week do you have a bet?

    (*tick one*)   less than once a week ....

                         1–3 times a week ....

                        over 3 times a week ....

If no to question 6
Do you have any friends who bet?

    (*tick one*)   yes ....

                                                  no ....

QUESTIONNAIRE A

In the following questions we would like you to tell us a little about yourself, your family and your friends. First we would like you to tell us something about yourself.

1 How old are you? I am

    (*tick one*)   14 yrs old ....

                                  15 yrs old ....

                                  16 yrs old ....

                                  17 yrs old ......✓............

                                  18 yrs old ....

                                  19 yrs old ....

2 Will you have left school by the end of next term?

    (*tick one*)   yes ....

                                                  no ......✓............

N<small>DS</small>

3 Which sex are you?
   (*tick one*)

                            male ....
                            female ....

4 How many brothers and sisters have you altogether?
   (*tick one*)

                            none ....
                            one ....
                            two ....
                            three ....
              more than three ....

5 Does anyone else sleep in the same room where you sleep?
   (*tick one*)

                            yes ....
                            no ....

6 Do you have a room to yourself at home in which to do your homework?
   (*tick one*)

                            yes ....
                            no ....

7 Tick which of the following people live in your house

                            father ....
                          mother ....
                        brothers ....
                          sisters ....
             aunts or uncles ....
                          cousins ....
                     stepfather ....
                  stepmother ....
                  other people ....

REMEMBER TO ANSWER EVERY QUESTION

8 What position would you say you hold in your form in general, that is, taking account of all your schools subjects, in comparison to others?

(*tick one*)

in the top five	....
in the top ten	........✓...........
just above the middle	....
below the middle	....

9 Have you ever been in trouble with the police?

(*tick one*)

yes	....	✓
no	.....✓.............	

10 *Only answer this question if you answered YES to question 9, otherwise go straight to question 11*
If yes to question 9
Have you ever been placed on probation?

(*tick one*)

yes	....
no	....

now go on to question 11

11 How many of your friends have been in trouble with the police?

(*tick one*)

none	....
less than five	........✓..........
five to ten	....
more than ten	....

REMEMBER TO ANSWER EVERY QUESTION

12 Children in their spare time after school and in the weekends do a lot of different things. Which of the following do *you* do at least *once a week*

    (*a*) watch television at home ....✓..........

    (*b*) listen to pop records ....✓..........

    (*c*) go out with the rest of the family ....

    (*d*) read a library book ....✓..........

    (*e*) go to a party ....✓..........

    (*f*) play sport for your school or club ....

    (*g*) go to the pictures ....✓..........

put a (*h*) sit around in a coffee bar ....✓..........

tick
next (*i*) go to a pub ....✓..........

to the (*j*) make models and things ....

ones
you do (*k*) help old people and others in need ....

at (*l*) sit at home with the rest of the family ....

least
once a (*m*) play chess ....✓..........

week (*n*) go out with the girls ....✓..........

    (*o*) go out with the boys ....✓..........

    (*p*) go to a youth club ....

    (*q*) do a part time job ....✓..........

    (*r*) go to Soho ....✓..........

    (*s*) work on a motor car or motor bike ....

    (*t*) go to a bowling alley ....

    (*u*) go dancing ....✓..........

13 With whom do you *usually* go out?

    (*tick one*)   with a group of boys and girls ....✓..........

    with adults ....

    with a girl friend ....

    with a group of boys ....✓

    alone ....

    with a boy friend ....

    with a group of girls ....

14 What is the total amount of money that you earn or are given to spend each week?

    (*tick one*)   less than 5*s* ....

                            5*s* to 10*s* ....

                          10*s* to £1 ....

                          £1 to £3 ....

                    more than £3 ......✓...........

15 With the money that you earn or are given to spend each week:

(i) *How much do you save?*

    (*tick one*)   all of it ....

                three-quarters of it ....

                    half of it ....

                 quarter of it ....

                    none of it ....✓...........

(ii) *How much do you spend on clothes?*

    (*tick one*)   all of it ....

                three-quarters of it ....

                    half of it ......✓...........

                 quarter of it ....

                    none of it ....

(iii) *How much do you spend on cigarettes, drugs and alcohol?*

    (*tick one*)   all of it ....

                three-quarters of it ....

                    half of it .....✓...........

                 quarter of it ....

                    none of it ....

REMEMBER YOUR ANSWERS ARE CONFIDENTIAL

Now we would like you to tell us a little more about yourself and your friends.

So please tell the truth but do not boast.

16 When you go out with your friends to some place where you can be alone with them how many of them will:

smoke cigarettes

(*tick one*)

all of them ....

half of them ....✓...............

quarter of them ....

none of them ....

17 *take drugs*

(*tick one*)

all of them ....

half of them ....

quarter of them .....✓..............

none of them ....

18 *drink alcohol*

(*tick one*)

all of them .....✓...............

half of them ....

quarter of them ....

none of them ....

19 In fact, how many boys and girls do you know who?

smoke

(*tick one*)

none ....

less than 5 ....

6–10 ....

11–50 ....✓.............

more than 50 ....

20 *take drugs*
   (*tick one*)

none	....
less than 5	....
6–10	...✓.............
11–50	....
more than 50	....

21 *drink alcohol*
   (*tick one*)

none	....
less than 5	....
6–10	....
11–50	.......✓...........
more than 50	....

22 Do you yourself ever smoke cigarettes?
   (*tick one*)

yes	........✓.............
no	....

*If you answered YES to question 22 then answer questions 23 and 24
otherwise go straight on to question 25
If yes to question 22*

23 Do you usually smoke filter-tipped cigarettes?
   (*tick one*)

yes	✓.....................
no	....

24 About how many cigarettes do you smoke?
   (*tick one*)
   (*a*) I have only tried a cigarette once ....
   (*b*) I only smoke occasionally ....
   (*c*) less than 5 cigarettes a week ....
   (*d*) 5–10 cigarettes a week ....
   (*e*) 10–20 cigarettes a week ....
   (*f*) 20 or more cigarettes a week ....✓.........

REMEMBER YOUR ANSWERS ARE CONFIDENTIAL

If no to question 22

25 How many times approximately have you been offered a cigarette and refused it?

> (*tick one*)

never	....
1–10 times	......✓...........
10–50 times	....
more than 50 times	....

Question 26 is to be answered by everyone

26 Have you yourself ever taken any drugs other than those prescribed by a doctor?

> (*tick one*)

yes	......✓...........
no	....

If you answered yes to question 26 then answer question 27 please, otherwise go straight on to question 28

If yes to question 26

27 Which of the following drugs have you taken and how many times have you taken them?

> (*Tick the appropriate squares*)

	Pep pills	Hashish or Marijuana	LSD	Heroin	Other
I have only taken this drug once	✓				
I have taken this drug less than 5 times			✓		
I sometimes take this drug at weekends or parties					
I take this drug 1–5 times a week		✓			✓
I take this drug more than 5 times a week					
I have now stopped taking this drug					

If no to question 26

28 How many times have you been offered drugs and refused them?

    (*tick one*)

        never ....

        1–10 times .... ✓

        10–50 times ....

        more than 50 times ....

Question 29 is to be answered by everyone

29 Have you yourself ever drunk alcohol other than at home?

    (*tick one*)

        yes .... ✓

        no ....

If you answered yes to question 29 then answer questions 30 and 31, otherwise go straight on to question 32

If yes to question 29

30 Which of the following have you drunk?

    (*tick the ones you have taken*)

        beer .... ✓

        cider .... ✓

        whisky .... ✓

        gin .... ✓

        vodka .... ✓

        wine .... ✓

        liqueur .... ✓

31 How many times do you have a drink?

    (*tick one*)   (a) I have only had a drink once ....

        (b) I have only had a few drinks ....

        (c) less than once a week ....

        (d) 1–5 times a week .... ✓

        (e) 5 or more times a week ....

REMEMBER YOUR ANSWERS ARE CONFIDENTIAL

If no to question 29

32 How many times approximately have you been offered a drink
and refused it?

(*tick one*)   never ....

1–10 times .....✓............

10–50 times ....

more than 50 times ....

ALL THE REMAINING QUESTIONS IN ALL QUESTION-
NAIRES ARE TO BE ATTEMPTED BY EVERYBODY

33 What is the name of your father's job?

....

34 Now describe carefully what he does.

....

....

35 What is the name of the job that *you* want to do when you
leave school?

....

....

36 What is the name of the job your *parents* want you to do when
you leave school?

....

....

37 When you have a personal problem with whom do you
usually talk it over?

(*tick one*)   your father ....

your mother ....

your brother or sister ....

your priest ....

another relative ....

an older person you know ....

a close friend of your own age ....

with no one ....

38 What social class do you think you and your family belong to?

(*tick one*)   upper middle class ....

middle class ....

lower middle class ....

upper working class ....

working class ....

no particular class ....

QUESTIONNAIRE B

People have different ideas about many things. For example, below are a list of ideas that some young people hold about themselves, their families and their friends.

You will agree with some of them and *disagree* with others. Sometimes you will *agree strongly* and at other times you will *disagree strongly*. Now and then you may be *uncertain* whether you agree or disagree.

Read each of these sentences carefully, then put a tick by it in the column which is right for *you*.

Remember to answer every question.

	Strongly agree	Agree	Un-certain	Dis-agree	Strongly disagree
1 I would like to have more close friends				✓	
2 My father is the most important person to me				✓	
3 I would like to know more people that I could share secrets with				✓	
4 My parents let me stay out to all hours	✓				
5 My mother is like a friend to me		✓			
6 My parents never let me do the things other teenagers do				✓	
7 The best way to be accepted by your friends is to be twice as good as they are at everything				✓	
8 I am allowed to go to all the parties I want to			✓		

9 My father was never there when I wanted him
☐ ☐ ☐ ☑ ☐

10 At home I can get away with anything
☐ ☐ ☐ ☑ ☐

11 My parents do not even let me choose my own clothes
☐ ☐ ☐ ☑ ☐

12 Teenagers are often very lonely people
☐ ☑ ☐ ☐ ☐

13 My mother is always there when I want her
☐ ☑ ☐ ☐ ☐

14 I always make up my own mind about things
☑ ☐ ☐ ☐ ☐

15 My parents gave me too much
☐ ☐ ☑ ☐ ☐

16 Adolescence is a difficult time to make friends
☐ ☐ ☐ ☑ ☐

17 I would like to be the sort of person my father is
☐ ☐ ☐ ☑ ☐

18 The loner has most freedom
☐ ☐ ☑ ☐ ☐

19 My mother never advises me on anything
☐ ☐ ☐ ☑ ☐

20 My parents always say I am not old enough to do things
☐ ☐ ☐ ☑ ☐

21 I would like to know more people of my own age
☐ ☐ ☐ ☑ ☐

22 I don't have much to do with my father ☐ ☐ ☐ ☑ ☐

23 My parents were not strict enough with me ☐ ☐ ☐ ☑ ☐

24 I was always stopped from doing what I wanted to do by my parents ☐ ☐ ☐ ☑ ☐

25 I don't find it easy to get on with people of my own age ☐ ☐ ☐ ☑ ☐

26 My mother is very close to me ☐ ☑ ☐ ☐ ☐

27 Parents don't think highly enough of their children ☐ ☑ ☐ ☐ ☐

28 When I was young my father was never around very much ☐ ☐ ☐ ☑ ☐

29 My parents don't like the job I want to do ☐ ☐ ☐ ☑ ☐

30 I am very self-confident ☐ ☑ ☐ ☐ ☐

31 My parents allow me to do too many things ☐ ☐ ☐ ☑ ☐

32 My mother is very important to me ☑ ☐ ☐ ☐ ☐

33 My parents don't allow me to do enough ☐ ☐ ☐ ☑ ☐

34 Parents ought to let children make up their own minds about jobs ☑ ☐ ☐ ☐ ☐

QUESTIONNAIRE C

We have below a number of statements about how young people feel about life in general. Each of these statements is paired with another. You have to choose which of the two statements in each pair you agree with most and then place a tick beside it.

Remember even though you may agree or disagree with both statements you tick only ONE of them—the one that is most right for *you*. Tick one statement in *every* pair.

1(*a*) A teenager should be liked by as many people as possible ....

 or

 (*b*) A teenager should not pay attention to what other people think ✓ ....

2(*a*) One should never get help from others with one's homework ....

 or

 (*b*) It doesn't matter who helps with one's homework as long as the teacher does not find out ✓ ....

3(*a*) If one finds a purse in the street one should always give it to a policeman ....

 or

 (*b*) Anything one finds in the street one should be able to keep for oneself ✓ ....

4(*a*) Life is too short to work ✓ ....

 or

 (*b*) Only foolish people do not work ....

5(*a*) What I would most like to do is to live a useful life ....

 or

 (*b*) What I most would like to do is earn lots of money ✓ ....

6(*a*) The police often pick on us for no good reason   ✓

or

(*b*) The police do a difficult job as well as they can   ....

7(*a*) Nothing can stop me when I make up my mind to do something   ....✓..........

or

(*b*) I always hesitate and listen to others before doing anything   ....

8(*a*) There is a lot of truth in what the Church says   ....

or

(*b*) Church is a waste of time   ....✓..........

9(*a*) Only squares are always on time   ....

or

(*b*) A person should always be on time   ....✓..........

10(*a*) Life is more fun when one does daring things   ....✓..........

or

(*b*) One should always be sure something is safe before one does it   ....

11(*a*) Any homework should always be done as best as you can do it   ....

or

(*b*) As long as the teacher says the homework is all right it does not matter how good you think it is   ....

12(*a*) One should never work too hard   ....

or

(*b*) Hard work can be a lot of fun   ....

13(*a*) A teenager should always try something
new   ....

   or

(*b*) A teenager should stick to the old and
trusted ways   ....

14(*a*) One should pay attention to those older
than yourself   ....

   or

(*b*) Young people know that older people are
often wrong   ....

15(*a*) One should never steal anything   ....

   or

(*b*) Sometimes it is all right to steal   ....

16(*a*) The best job is one that pays a lot of
money   ....

   or

(*b*) The best job to have is where one can
draw or write   ....

17(*a*) The thing to do is to live as if today
was the last day one had to live   ....

   or

(*b*) One should always plan for the future   ....

QUESTIONNAIRE D

You have already told us about the things you do in your spare time. Now we would like to know *what kind of person* you are.

Here is a practice question about the kind of person you are.

Dare to take risks ☐ ☐ ☐ Want to be safe

If you are the kind of person who *dares to take risks*, put a tick in the box on the LEFT.

If you are the kind of person who *wants to be safe* put a tick in the box on the RIGHT.

Most people know which of these two kinds of person they are. But if you really cannot decide which kind of person *you* are, put a tick in the box in the MIDDLE.

That question was just for practice. Now put a tick by each of these questions in the box which is right for *the kind of person you are*.

1 Good at school work	☐	☐	☐	Not so good at school work
2 Interested in the opposite sex	☐	☐	☐	Not interested in the opposite sex
3 Good at sports	☐	☐	☐	Not good at sports
4 Gentle	☐	☐	☐	Tough
5 Often dis-obedient	☐	☐	☐	Usually do as I am told
6 Like to be alone	☐	☐	☐	Like to be with a group
7 A good fighter	☐	☐	☐	Not much of a fighter

8 Try to act 'big' ☐ ☐ ☐ Act my own age

9 Plan and think ahead ☐ ☐ ☐ Cannot wait, want everything at once

10 Have many friends ☐ ☐ ☐ Have one or two friends

11 Scruffy ☐ ☐ ☐ Neat and clean

12 A bit of a bully ☐ ☐ ☐ Do not bully

13 Like to do forbidden things ☐ ☐ ☐ Do not like to do forbidden things

14 Want to be grown up ☐ ☐ ☐ Do not yet want to be grown up

15 Sometimes swear ☐ ☐ ☐ Do not swear

16 Spend my money ☐ ☐ ☐ Save my money

17 Often successful ☐ ☐ ☐ Often a failure

18 Try to attract the opposite sex ☐ ☐ ☐ Do not try to attract the opposite sex

19 A bit of a cissy ☐ ☐ ☐ Tough

QUESTIONNAIRE E

You have told us about the kind of person you are really like. Here is something different. Think now about

THE KIND OF PERSON YOU WOULD LIKE TO BE

We want you to answer some of the same questions as before. But this time we are asking you about *the kind of person you would like to be*. This may not be the same as the kind of person you really are. So think carefully again about each question and then put a tick in the box which is right for *the kind of person you would like to be*.

1 Good at school work	☐	☐	☐	Not so good at school work
2 Interested in the opposite sex	☐	☐	☐	Not interested in the opposite sex
3 Good at sports	☐	☐	☐	Not good at sports
4 Gentle	☐	☐	☐	Tough
5 Often dis-obedient	☐	☐	☐	Usually do as I am told
6 Like to be alone	☐	☐	☐	Like to be with a group
7 A good fighter	☐	☐	☐	Not much of a fighter
8 Try to act 'big'	☐	☐	☐	Act my own age
9 Plan and think ahead	☐	☐	☐	Cannot wait, want everything at once

10 Have many friends	☐	☐	☐	Have one or two friends
11 Scruffy	☐	☐	☐	Neat and clean
12 A bit of a bully	☐	☐	☐	Do not bully
13 Like to do forbidden things	☐	☐	☐	Do not like to do forbidden things
14 Want to be grown up	☐	☐	☐	Do not yet want to be grown up
15 Sometimes swear	☐	☐	☐	Do not swear
16 Spend my money	☐	☐	☐	Save my money
17 Often successful	☐	☐	☐	Often a failure
18 Try to attract the opposite sex	☐	☐	☐	Do not try to attract the opposite sex
19 A bit of a cissy	☐	☐	☐	Tough

QUESTIONNAIRE F

Below are a number of statements about drugs. Some are TRUE and some are FALSE.

If you think a statement is correct then put a tick next to it in the column TRUE.

If you think the statement is not true then put a tick in the column FALSE.

If you do not know whether the statement is correct or not, then put a tick in the column DON'T KNOW.

Remember your answers are confidential so please answer every question as truthfully as you can.

	True	False	Don't know
1 The only way one can take LSD is on a sugar lump		✓	
2 Marijuana is made from the same plant as heroin		✓	
3 Heroin costs about 20s a grain on the black market			
4 Tolerance means that one comes to like a drug the more one takes it		✓	
5 Many adults are dependent upon barbiturates	✓		
6 LSD tastes like milk		✓	
7 Pep pills help to keep you awake	✓		
8 Withdrawal symptoms come when one takes too big a dose of a drug		✓	
9 LSD always gives one hallucinations		✓	
10 A reefer is cheaper to buy than a grain of heroin	✓		

11 Everyone always gets the same effects from a drug ☐ ☑ ☐

12 Heroin at first often makes you sick ☑ ☐ ☐

13 LSD is the only known psychedelic drug ☐ ☑ ☐

14 As soon as one has some heroin one is hooked on it ☑ ☐ ☐

15 Physical addiction means that one's body comes to need the drug ☑ ☐ ☐

16 LSD has the same effect every time it is taken ☐ ☑ ☐

17 Beginners do not always enjoy marijuana ☑ ☐ ☐

18 No pep pills are addictive ☑ ☐ ☐

19 Marijuana and hashish are different preparations from the same plant ☑ ☑ ☐

20 The only way one can take heroin is by injecting it ☐ ☑ ☐

21 One can take as many pep pills as one likes with no ill effects ☐ ☑ ☐

22 Marijuana can be cooked and eaten as a sweetmeat ☑ ☐ ☐

23 Heroin is never taken in combination with any other drug ☐ ☑ ☐

24 Mescalin is another name for marijuana ☐ ☑ ☐

25 Once you start taking pep pills you can't stop

26 LSD was first manufactured in Switzerland

27 Cigarettes and alcohol are drugs

28 Marijuana usually affects you so much that other people might think you were mad

29 'Four and four' is a term used by doctors when referring to the number of male and female addicts

30 Immediately one takes LSD spectacular things happen

31 Drug dependency means that one's life is centred around drugs

32 Marijuana is used by a large number of GPs to make patients well

33 No one can tell by any means whatever whether you have taken a pep pill or not

34 Hashish is normally cut up and smoked

35 All pep pills look the same

36 Once you start taking heroin regularly you keep needing more and more to get any kick

37 Marijuana is made from the same plant as hashish

38 A heroin-taker often starts off with one-sixth of a grain

39 Cannabis looks more like LSD than marijuana ☐ ☑ ☐

40 Phyceptone is addictive ☐ ☐ ☐

41 Amphetamines do not have the same effect as barbiturates ☑ ☐ ☐

42 Like anything else, one needs a lot of LSD before it has any effect ☐ ☑ ☐

43 Psilocybin is a pep pill ☐ ☐ ☐

44 Heroin is grown on a heroin tree ☐ ☑ ☐

45 LSD is colourless, tasteless and odourless ☐ ☑ ☐

46 Marijuana can only be taken by injection ☐ ☑ ☐

This section also concerns drugs. This time instead of a statement there is a list of words. Each of these words is more commonly used with 1 of 4 particular drugs.

After each word there is column space for each of these four drugs. You must put a tick in the column of the drug that you think each word refers to.

Remember to answer every question.

First word 'purple heart' is done for you.

	Pep pill	Heroin	LSD	Marijuana	Don't know
47 purple heart	☑	☐	☐	☐	☐
48 flushing	☐	☐	☐	☐	☐

49 hash

50 drinamyl

51 jacks

52 black bomber

53 guide

54 resin

55 cold turkey

56 sugar

57 spliff

58 mainliner

59 hallucinogenic

60 acid

61 pill head

62 grain

63 dexies

□ □ □ □ □

64 weed

□ □ □ □ □

65 trip

□ □ □ □ □

66 durophet

□ □ □ □ □

67 reefer

□ □ □ □ □

CHECK THAT YOU HAVE PLACED A TICK IN THE RIGHT
COLUMN BESIDE EVERY WORD

QUESTIONNAIRE G

People have different ideas about many things. For example below are listed a number of ideas that young people hold about drugs. You will AGREE with some of them and DISAGREE with others. Sometimes you will AGREE STRONGLY and at other times you will DISAGREE STRONGLY. Now and then you may be UNCERTAIN whether you agree or disagree.

Read each of the statements carefully, then put a tick by it in the column which is right for you.

Remember your answers are confidential so please tell the truth and *answer every question*.

	Strongly agree	Agree	Un-certain	Dis-agree	Strongly disagree
1 Drugs are all right if only taken occasionally	✓				
2 Drugs are an aid to creative people	✓				
3 You can't trust drug-takers				✓	
4 Drugs are not as dangerous as newspapers make out	✓				
5 Drugs can make you a fuller person	✓				
6 Smoking is more dangerous than taking drugs	✓				
7 Only if you take drugs can you make the London scene				✓	
8 Drugs will make you mad				✓	

9 Not enough is known about drugs to make them safe

10 It is safer to drive with someone on pot rather than with someone drunk on alcohol

11 Drugs are good because they make you self-confident

12 The risk of heroin hooking you is over-exaggerated

13 It would be fine to take drugs if it were not for the police

14 Drugs are a valuable new experience

15 Only fools get hooked on drugs

16 Pep pills are great for kicks

17 Drugs are all right if one doesn't take alcohol at the same time

QUESTIONNAIRE H

Now we would like you to tell us a little about
THE KINDS OF PEOPLE WHO TAKE DRUGS

This is similar to the questionnaires you have answered
before about yourself and the one about the kind of person
you would like to be.

But this time we are asking you about the kind of person *who
takes drugs*. So think carefully about each question and then put a
tick in the box which is right for what you think of the kind of
people *who take drugs*.

1 Good at school work	☑	☐	☐	Not so good at school work
2 Interested in the opposite sex	☑	☐	☐	Not interested in the opposite sex
3 Good at sports	☐	☐	☐	Not good at sports
4 Gentle	☐	☐	☐	Tough
5 Often dis-obedient	☐	☐	☐	Usually does as he is told
6 Like to be alone	☐	☐	☐	Like to be with a group
7 A good fighter	☐	☐	☐	Not much of a fighter
8 Try to act 'big'	☐	☐	☐	Acts his own age
9 Plan and think ahead	☐	☐	☐	Cannot wait, want everything at once

10 Have many friends	□	□	□	Have one or two friends
11 Scruffy	□	□	□	Neat and clean
12 A bit of a bully	□	□	□	Do not bully
13 Like to do forbidden things	□	□	□	Do not like to do forbidden things
14 Want to be grown up	□	□	□	Do not yet want to be grown up
15 Sometimes swear	□	□	□	Do not swear
16 Spends his money	□	□	□	Saves his money
17 Often successful	□	□	□	Often a failure
18 Try to attract the opposite sex	□	□	□	Do not try to attract the opposite sex
19 A bit of a cissy	□	□	□	Tough

QUESTIONNAIRE I

Listed below are the first words in a number of sentences. We would like you to complete each of these sentences. Write as quickly as you can and do not spend too much time on any one question.

1 I am most nervous ....
....
....

2 The first time I took drugs ....
....
....

3 To be tolerant ....
....
....

4 Drugs are called by many different names, some of these are
....
....

5 Looking back on all the times I have taken drugs, I think ......
.... Good for me ....
....

6 I think the world will end in ..... when I am dead
....
....

7 I think it is likely that in the future ....
....
....

8 I wish my friends would ....
....
....

QUESTIONNAIRE J

1 In your opinion how many pupils in your school:
   (a) smoke ....400.....
   (b) take drugs ....25.......
   (c) drink alcohol ....700..

2 Please write any comments that you have about the questionnaire that you have just completed.

   ....
   ....
   ....
   ....
   ....
   ....
   ....
   ....
   ....

APPENDIX E

Letters and instructions

1 LETTER TO THE LOCAL EDUCATION AUTHORITY

Dear ———

I am carrying out a social survey of drug-taking habits and attitudes to drug-taking among children of school leaving age.

As you will know, drug-taking is said to be on the increase in the general population as a whole and amidst school children in particular. However there are so far few objective measures of the actual incidence of drug-taking and it is of course difficult to know without this, what sort of action should be taken. One of the aims of this survey is to provide in part, such an objective measure.

Whatever the case, it is apparent that in the near future some campaign will have to be undertaken by those responsible to warn children of the dangers of drug-taking. This can only be done if one is already aware of how much information children have and the attitudes which they hold towards drug-takers. Another aim of the survey is to find this out.

The initial stage of the survey has already been completed. This involved giving a series of questionnaires to a small sample of school leavers attending comprehensive schools. The aim of that stage was to develop the necessary, precise research tools. In the next and main stage of the survey, schools will be needed from different L.E.A. areas.

If you are agreeable I should like to write to the principals of a number of schools in your area to ask if I could come and discuss the research with them. It is hoped to complete the arrangements with them during the first half of the Michaelmas term so that the work may be carried out during the last weeks of the term. The study is of course strictly confidential and no schools or pupils will be named.

I should be most grateful if you would agree to this request.

Yours sincerely, R. Wiener B.A.

2 LETTER TO THE PROBATION OFFICERS

Dear ————

I am carrying out a social survey of drug-taking habits and attitudes to drug-taking among children of school leaving age in your area.

I have found that other probation officers have been most helpful in providing a background picture of the drug-taking pattern as they perceive it in their area. This information has of course been treated in the strictest confidence.

I wonder whether it might be possible to come and see you to discuss the nature of my research and its application to your area. I will phone you early next week to see if a time can be found which is convenient for you.

Yours faithfully, R. Wiener B.A.

3 LETTER TO THE HEADMASTER

Dear ————

I am carrying out a social survey of drug-taking among children of school leaving age. As you will know there have been various reports testifying to the rumoured widespread incidence of drug-taking in the population as a whole and among school children in particular. One of the essential requisites is to obtain an objective measure of the incidence so as to be able to place the subjective reports in their true perspective.

Whatever the case it is apparent that in the near future some campaign will have to be undertaken by those responsible to warn children of the dangers of drug-taking. This can only be done if one is already aware of how much information children have and the attitudes which they hold towards drug-takers. Another aim of this survey is to find this out.

The initial stage of the survey has already been completed. This involved giving a series of questionnaires to a small sample of school leavers attending comprehensive schools. The aim of that stage was to develop the necessary, precise research tools.

The next and main stage of the survey will only involve pupils who are known to be leaving school during the coming academic year. Pupils will be needed from schools drawn from different educational boroughs. The Local Education Authority has agreed that the research may be conducted in schools in your area. Your school has been selected for the sample and I should be most grateful if you would permit the work to be carried out there. For this much needed survey to be successful it is essential for all schools in the sample to participate and the success of our work is therefore dependent upon the cooperation of individual headmasters. Any information we obtain is treated as strictly confidential and the name of the school will not be mentioned in the report of the results. It is not necessary for us to know the names of the children who take part.

We would prefer the children not to have any previous information about the subject matter of the survey as this can influence their replies and I should be obliged if you could ask any members of your staff whose timetables might be interrupted not to mention the main purpose of our visit to the children.

It is hoped to commence the survey in the first weeks of next term. We would therefore like to complete the preliminary arrangements for the survey by the end of November. Would it therefore be possible to come and call on you during October to see if you would be prepared to assist in the survey, and, if you were, to discuss arrangements with you. Perhaps you could let me have a time and date, preferably a range of dates, when this would be convenient for you.

I would be most grateful for your cooperation.

Your sincerely, R. Wiener B.A.

4 INSTRUCTIONS TO THE SUBJECTS

Good morning/afternoon. My name is ——. We come from the London School of Economics. Part of our work there is to do surveys about the way different people live and the opinions they have. Sometimes we are interested in adults and sometimes in young people like yourselves. Today we are going to ask you some questions about yourselves, about what you do in your spare time and also about what you think of various things.

This is not a test or an exam and we are not worried about bad spelling or crossings out.

Do not open your questionnaires yet.

This survey is completely confidential. Nobody in this school is going to see your answers. As soon as you have finished, these questionnaires will be placed in these big envelopes and sealed. They will then be taken and placed in a big computer. Just to show you how confidential your answers are going to be we will not ask you to put your name on the questionnaire. Therefore neither your teachers, your parents or anybody else will ever be able to know what you have written. Therefore be as frank and honest as you can. Just answer as truthfully as you can and no one will ever know that you said it.

Now it is important for this survey for each person to give their answers to the questions and not someone else's. There must therefore be no talking or trying to look at what someone else has written. Remember that there are no right and wrong answers. If you have any difficulties just raise your hand. Don't be afraid to ask. It's quite possible that we have not made one or two of the questions quite clear.

Now look at the top page of the questionnaires. You will see it is headed 'kinds of questions'. These are examples of the types of questions that you will have to answer.

Look at number 1. In this type of question you are asked to tick one of a number of alternative answers. In this question the person who answered watches television on three evenings a week and so he placed a tick next to the number 'three' in the answers. Some questions might ask you to tick more than one answer so read each question carefully.

Now look at the second type of question. Here there are two sentences together. You are asked to choose which one you agree with most. You must always choose one from each pair of sentences and place a tick beside it. If, for example, you thought cricket was an interesting rather than a boring sport, you would place a tick next to the first sentence.

Now look at the third type of question. In this case you are asked to look at a pair of words to see which word best describes yourself or some other type of person. Read this type of question carefully when you come to it to make sure who the person is that you have to describe. In this answer the person felt that he was nice rather than nasty so he placed a tick next to the word 'nice'.

Now look at question 4. Here there is a statement: 'Footballers are great people.' You have to choose from alternative answers.

You have to decide whether you agree strongly with the statement when you place a tick under the column headed *Strongly agree*, or, whether though you agree that footballers are great people you do not feel particularly strongly about it. In this case you place a tick under the column headed *Agree*. Or you might disagree that footballers are great people, when you place your tick in the column headed *Disagree*, or you might disagree strongly, when you place your tick in the column headed *Strongly Disagree*. Only place a tick in the *Uncertain* column if you really cannot decide how you feel about a particular statement. In the example in front of you the person agreed that footballers were great people but he didn't feel particularly strongly about it and therefore placed a tick in the *Agree* column.

Now questions like question 5 are simple. All they ask is whether you think a statement is true or false. In question 5, for example, if you thought that Noah did build the ark you would place a tick in the *True* column.

Now look finally at question 6. This type of question has two parts. In the first part you have to answer yes or no to a question. In this example you place a tick beside the 'yes' if you have had a bet and beside the 'no' if you have not had a bet. Now look at the second part. You will see one section headed *if yes,* and one section *if no*. Now if you answered yes to the first part of the question then in the second part you answer the question under *if yes*. If you answered no to the first part then you answer only the question under *if no*. You only answer one of the sections.

These are examples of the types of questions that you have to answer. You see they are not difficult. But remember if you have any trouble, if you are not sure how to answer a question then just raise your hand. Remember to answer every question and remember that neither your teachers, your parents or anyone but the computer will read your answers. So please be as truthful as you can. There are no right and wrong answers and it is important for each person to give their own answers.

Now there are nine questionnaires to get through so work as quickly as you can and do not spend too long on any one question. When you have finished one questionnaire go on to the next one till you have finished. When you have finished raise your hand.

Now are there any questions? Right, now turn to Questionnaire A.

Bibliography

1. DRUGS, DEVIANCE AND SOCIAL ACTIVITIES OF YOUNG PEOPLE

ADDICTION RESEARCH UNIT, see Kosviner *et al.* [126]

ALARCON, R. DE and RATHOD, N. H. (1968) 'Prevalence and early detection of heroin abuse', *Br. Med. J.*, 1 June, 549–53. [1]

ANDREWS, G., VINKENOOG, S. and OWEN, P. (1967) *The Book of Grass: an anthology on Indian Hemp*, Peter Owen Ltd. [2]

AUSUBEL, D. P. (1958) *Drug Addiction: Physiological, Psychological and Sociological Aspects*, New York, Random House. [3]

AUSUBEL, D. P. (1966) 'Controversial issues in the management of drug addiction', in O'Donnell and Ball (162). [4]

BALL, J. C. (1965) 'Two patterns of narcotic drug abuse in the United States', *The Journal of Criminal Law*, Criminology & Police Sc., 56, No. 21. [5]

BALL, J. C. (1967) 'The reliability and validity of interview data obtained from 59 narcotic drug addicts', *Am. J. Sociol.*, 72, 6, 650–4. [6]

BALL, J. C. and O'DONNELL, J. A. (1966) 'Selected social characteristics of consecutive admissions to Lexington', *Criminologica*, 4, No. 2. [7]

BANDURA, A. and WALTERS, R. H. (1963) *Social Learning and Personality Development*, New York, Holt, Rinehart & Winston. [8]

BARRIGAR, R. H. (1964) 'The regulation of psychedelic drugs', *Psychedelic Review*, 1, 394–441. [9]

BARWELL, T. (1967) *Drugs and delinquent behaviour*, unpub. report to Chief Psychologist, Prison Dept, Home Office, July. [10]

BBC (British Broadcasting Corporation) (1966) 'A talk on marijuana', Radio Three, November. [11]

BECKER, H. S. (1963) *Outsiders: Studies in the Sociology of deviancy*, New York, Free Press of Glencoe. [12]

BECKETT, D. (1968) 'The Salter Unit—an experimental in-patient treatment centre for narcotic drug addiction', *Br. J. Addict*, 63, 51–3. [13]

BELL, D. S. and TRETHOWAN, W. H. (1961) 'Amphetamine Addiction', *J. Nerv. Ment. Dis.*, 1961, 133, 489–96. [14]

BENDER, L. (1966) 'D-Lysergic acid in the treatment of the biological features of childhood schizophrenia, *Dis. Nerv. Syst.* (Suppl.) 27, 543–6. [15]

BENUSIGLIO, D., KOSVINER, A., PIXNER, S., STIMSON, G. and ZACUNE, J. (1967) 'Soft, hard and psychedelic, unpub. report, London School of Economics. [16]

BESTIC, A. (1966) *Turn Me On Man*, Library 33 Ltd. [17]

BEWLEY, T. (1965) 'Recent changes in the pattern on drug abuse in the United Kingdom', *Bulletin on Narcotics*, 18, No. 4. [18]

BEWLEY, T. (1965) 'Heroin and cocaine addiction', *Lancet*, 10 April, 808–10. [19]

BEWLEY, T. (1965) 'Heroin addiction in the United Kingdom (1954–64)', *Br. Med. J.*, 2, 1284–6. [20]

BEWLEY, T. (1965) Memorandum: Prescribing clinics for the treatment of drug addicts, personal communication. [21]

BEWLEY, T. (1968) 'The Diagnosis and Management of Heroin Addiction', *Practitioner*, 200, 215–20. [22]

BINNIE, L. and MURDOCK, G. (1969) 'The attitudes to drugs and drug takers of students at the university and colleges of higher education in an English midland city', unpub. report. [23]

BLUM, R. *et al.* (1965) *Utopiates: The Use and Users of LSD 25*, Tavistock. [24]

BOWLBY, J. (1965) *Child Care and the Growth of Love*, Penguin Books, 2nd edn. [25]

BRADLEY, P. and KEY, B. (1963) 'Conditioning Experiments with LSD', in Crockett, R. A. and Sandison, R. A., op. cit. [26]

BREAM, H. (1965) 'A Global Criminal Trade', in *Time/Life* Special Report, op. cit. [27]

BRILL, L. (1965) 'After-care rehabilitation', in Harms, E., op. cit. [28]

British Broadcasting Corporation, see BBC.

British Medical Journal (1967) Leading article, 8 April. [29]

British Medical Journal (1967) Leading article, 20 April. [30]

Bulletin on Narcotics (1962) 'Note: An experiment in the supervision of parolled offenders addicted to narcotic drugs', 14, April–June. [31]

Bulletin on Narcotics (1962) 'The cannabis problem: a note on the problem and the history of international action', 14, Oct.–Dec. [32]

BURROUGHS, W. (1959) *The Naked Lunch*, Paris, Olympia Press. [33]

CAMERON, D. C. (1963) 'Addiction: current issues', *Am. J. Psychiat.*, 120, 313–19. [34]

CAMERON, K. (1963) 'Some experiences with LSD in the treatment of adolescent boys', in Delay, J., op. cit. [35]

CANTERI, C. (1968) Personal communication. [36]

CAREY, S. (1968) Personal communication. [37]

CARR, A. J. (1965) 'Smoking in teenage girls', *Nursing Times*, **61**, 12 Feb., 225–7. [38]

CARSTAIRS, G. M. (1954) 'Daru and Bhang. Cultural factors in the choice of intoxicants', *Quart. J. Stud. Alc.*, **15**, 220–37. [39]

CARTWRIGHT, A., THOMSON, J. G., *et al.* (1960) 'An attitude study among school children touching also on parental influence', *Br. J. Preventive and Social Med.*, **14**, 28–34. [40]

CARTWRIGHT, R. D. (1966) 'Dream and drug-induced fantasy behaviour. A comparative study', *Arch. Gen. Psychiat.*, **15**, 1, 7–15. [41]

CHAPPLE, P. A. L. (1966) Letter to the editor, *Lancet*, 12 Feb. [42]

CHAPPLE, P. A. L. and GRAY, G. (1968), 'One year's work at a centre for the treatment of addicted patients', *Lancet*, 27 April, 908–11. [43]

CHEIN, I. (1956) 'Narcotics use among juveniles', *Social Work*, 1. [44]

CHEIN, I., GERARD, D. L., LEE, R. S. and ROSENFELD, E. (1964) *Narcotics, Delinquency and Social Policy: The Road to H.*, Tavistock. [45]

CHERKAS, M. S. (1965) 'Synanon Foundation: A radical approach to the problem of addiction', *Am. J. of Psychiat.*, **121**, 11, 1065–8. [46]

CLAUSON, J. (1954) 'Certain effects of mescaline and lysergic acid on psychological functions', *J. Psychol.*, **38**. [47]

COHEN, A. K. (1955) *Delinquent Boys, the Culture of the Gang*, New York, Free Press of Glencoe. [48]

COHEN, A. K. (1966) *Deviance and Control*, New York, Prentice-Hall. [49]

COHEN, S. (1965) *Drugs of Hallucination*, Secker & Warburg. [50]

COHEN, S. (1965) 'Drugs that mimic madness', in *Time/Life* Special Report, op. cit. [51]

COHEN, S. and DITMAN, K. S. (1963) 'Prolonged adverse reactions to LSD', *Arch. Gen. Psychiat.*, **8**, 475–80. [52]

CONNELL, P. H. (1964) 'What to do about pep pills', *New Society*, 20 Feb. [53]

CONNELL, P. H. (1964) 'Amphetamine misuse', *Br. J. Addict.*, **60**, No. 1, 9–27. [54]

CONNELL, P. H. (1967) 'Importance of research', *Br. Med. J.*, 20 May. [55]

CONNELL, P. H. (1968) 'The use and abuse of amphetamines', *Practitioner*, **200**, 234–43. [56]

COUNCIL ON MENTAL HEALTH (1969) 'Marijuana and society', *J.A.M.A.*, **204**, 1181. [57]

CROCKETT, R., SANDISON, R. A. and WALK, A. (1963) *Hallucinogenic drugs and their psychotherapeutic use: Proceedings of the Royal Medico-Psychological Association Feb. 1961*, Illinois, Charles C. Thomas. [58]

QDS

CURR, W., HALLWORTH, H. J. and WILKINSON, A. H. (1962) 'How secondary modern school children spend their time', *Ed. Review*, **15**, 3–9. [59]

Daily Express (1968) 'Drugs: How many are hooked', 4 June. [60]

Dangerous Drugs Acts (*a*) 1965, and (*b*) 1967. H.M.S.O. [61]

DAVIES, E. B. (1967) *Memorandum on the problem of Illicit Drug-taking and Dependence particularly among young people*. Based upon a lecture given to Heads of Secondary Schools in Cambridgeshire and the Isle of Ely on 16 March 1967, Cambridgeshire and Isle of Ely County Council. [62]

DEEDES, M. (1968) Report of speech in Parliament, *The Times*, 1 June. [63]

DELAY, J. *et al.* (1963) 'The therapeutic implications of psilocybin', in Crocket *et al.*, op. cit. [64]

DEROPP, R. S. (1958) *Drugs and the Mind*, Gollancz. [65]

Drugs (prevention of misuse) Act 1964. H.M.S.O. [66]

EDDY, N. and ISBELL, H. (1965) 'Drug dependence: its significance and characteristics', *Bull. Wld. Hlth. Org.*, **32**, No. 5, 721–33. [67]

EDUCATION AND SCIENCE, DEPARTMENT OF (1968) *A Handbook of Health Education*, H.M.S.O. [68]

EDWARDS, G. (1967) 'Relevance of American experience of narcotic addiction to the British scene', *Br. Med. J.*, 12 Aug., 425–9. [69]

EDWARDS, G. (1968) 'The problem of cannabis dependence', *Practitioner*, **200**, 226–33. [70]

EIDUSON, S., GELLER, E., YUWILER, A. and EIDUSON, B. (1964) *Biochemistry and Behaviour*, Van Nostrand. [71]

EINSTEIN, S. (1965) 'The future time perspective of the adolescent narcotic addict', in Harms, E., op. cit. [72]

EINSTEIN, S. and JONES, F. (1965) 'Group therapy with adolescent drug addicts', in Harms. E., op. cit. [73]

Evening Standard (1968) 'Schools alert—watch for drug takers', 3 May. [74]

FEINBERG, I. (1962) 'Schizophrenic versus mescaline and LSD hallucinations', in West, L. J. *Hallucinations*, Grune & Stratton. [75]

FIDDLE, S. (1967) *Portraits from a Shooting Gallery: Life Styles from the Drug Addict World*, New York, Harper & Row. [76]

FINESTONE, H. (1966) 'Narcotics and Criminality', in O'Donnell and Ball., op. cit. [77]

FINK, P. J., GOLDMAN, M. J. and LYONS, I. W. (1966) 'Morning Glory psychosis', *Arch. Gen. Psychiat.* **15**, 209–12. [78]

FINK, P., SIMEON, J., HAQUE, W. and ITIL, T. (1966) 'Prolonged adverse reactions to LSD in psychotic subjects', *Arch. Gen. Psychiat.*, **15**, 450–5. [79]

FORT, J. (1966) 'Heroin addiction among young men', in O'Donnell and Ball, op. cit. [80]

FORT, J. (1967) 'Recommended future international action against abuses of alcohol and other drugs', *Br. J. Addict.*, **62**, No. 1/2, 129–46. [81]

FRANKAU, LADY and STANWELL, P. (1960) 'The treatment of drug addiction', *Lancet*, 24 Dec., 1377–9. [82]

FREUD, S. (1963) *The Cocaine Papers*, Vienna, Dunquin Press. [83]

GANGE, ROSLYN and SHEEGART, G. (1966) 'The heroin addict's pseudo-assertive behaviour and family dynamics', *Social Caseworker*, Dec. [84]

GARMANY, G. (1968) 'Addiction to heroin', *Broadway*, Westminster Hospital J., June. [85]

GEBER, BERYL (1968) 'Analysis of use of amphetamines in a sample of non dependent drug users', unpub. paper. [86]

GERALD, D. L. and KORNETSKY, C. H. (1955) 'Adolescent opiate addiction: A study of control and addict subjects', *Psychiat. Quart.*, **29**, 457–86. [87]

GIBBENS, T. C. (1965) 'The misuse of drugs', *Howard J. of Penology*, 4. [88]

GILLESPIE, D., GLATT, M. M., HILLS, D. R. and PITTMAN, D. J. (1967) 'Drug dependence and abuse in England', *Br. J. Addict.*, **62**, No. 1/2, 155–70. [89]

GLATT, M. M. (1962) 'The abuse of barbiturates in the United Kingdom', *Bull. on Narcotics*, **14**, April–June. [90]

GLATT, M. M. (1968) 'Recent patterns of abuse and dependence on drugs', *Br. J. of Addict.*, **63**, No. 1/2, 111–28. [91]

GOLD, M. (1963) *Status Forces in Delinquent Boys*, Institute of Social Research, Univ. of Michigan. [92]

GOLDBERG, L. (1968) 'Drug abuse in Sweden 1', *Bull. on Narcotics*, **20**, Jan.–March. [93]

GOLDBERG, L. (1968) 'Drug abuse in Sweden 2', *Bull. on Narcotics*, **20**, April–June. [94]

GOVERNMENT SOCIAL SURVEY (1968) *Smoking among schoolboys*, Report S.S. 383 by J. M. Bynner, H.M.S.O. [95]

GREEN, W J. (1965) 'The effects of LSD on the sleep dream cycle', *J. Nerv. Ment. Dis.*, **140**, 417–26. [96]

GROOT, M. H. DE (1963) 'The role of hallucinogens in depersonalisation and allied syndromes', in Delay, *et al.*, op. cit. [97]

HALL, H., HAERTGER, C. A. and GLASERR, R. (1960) 'Personality characteristics of narcotic addicts as indicated by the M.M.P.I.', *J. Gen. Psychol.*, **62**, 127-39. [**98**]

HARMS, E. (1965) *Drug Addiction in Youth*, Pergamon Press: Inter. Series of Monographs on Child Psychiatry, vi. [**99**]

HAWKS, D., MITCHESON, M., OGBORNE, A. and EDWARDS, G. (1969) 'The abuse of methylamphetamine', *Br. Med. J.*, in press. [**100**]

HEALTH, MINISTRY OF, AND DEPARTMENT OF HEALTH FOR SCOTLAND (1961) *Drug Addiction. Report of the Interdepartmental Committee*, H.M.S.O. [**101**]

HEALTH, MINISTRY OF, AND DEPARTMENT OF HEALTH FOR SCOTLAND (1965) *Drug Addiction. The Second Report of the Interdepartmental Committee*, H.M.S.O. [**102**]

HEKIMAN, L. J. and GERSHON, G. (1968) 'Characteristics of drug abusers admitted to a psychiatric hospital', *J.A.M.A.*, **205**, 3. [**103**]

HERSOV, A. (1960) 'Refusal to go to school', *J. Child. Psych. and Psychiat.* **1**, No. 2, 137-45. [**104**]

HEWETSON, J. and OLLENDORF, R. (1964) 'Preliminary survey of one hundred London heroin and cocaine addicts', *Br. J. Addict.*, **60**, 109-14. [**105**]

HILTON, MARGARET (1968) 'Marijuana: A summary of the literature, Dissertation submitted in part fulfilment of the degree of B.A.', Sheffield University. [**106**]

HOFFER, A. (1967) 'Psychedelic experiences and the law', *Chitty's Law Journal*, **15**, No. 6. [**107**]

HOLDEN, H. M. (1966) 'Rebels without a cause', *Mental Health*, Autumn. [**108**]

HOME OFFICE, Report by the Advisory Committee on Drug Dependence (1968) *Cannabis*, H.M.S.O. [**109**]

HOME OFFICE (1968) '1967 Statistics for drug addiction and drug offences', Press release 1968. [**110**]

HOSPITAL CENTRE CONFERENCE, THE (1968) 'Treating drug dependency', *Nursing Times*, 17 May, 657. [**111**]

HOWELL, D. (1968) Report of speech in Parliament, *The Times*, 1 June [**112**]

HOWELL, D. (1967) Report of Question time in Parliament. *Lancet*, 9 Dec. [**113**]

HUGHES, H. MACGILL (1961) *The Fantastic Lodge,* Arthur Barker. [**114**]

HUXLEY, A. (1954) *Doors of Perception*, Chatto & Windus. [**115**]

HUXLEY, A. (1956) *Heaven and Hell*, Chatto & Windus. [**116**]

ISBELL, H. (1961) 'Perspective research on opiate addiction', *Br. J. Addict.*, **57**, No. 1, 17–30. [**117**]

ISBELL, H. (1966) 'Medical aspects of opiate addiction', in O'Donnell and Ball, op. cit. [**118**]

ISBELL, H. and WHITE, W. (1953) 'Clinical characteristics of addicts', *Am. J. Medicine*, **12**, No. 5. 558–61. [**119**]

JAFFE, J. J. (1956) 'Drug addiction and drug abuse', in GOODMAN, L. S. and GILMAN, A. (eds). *The Pharmacological Basis of Therapeutics*, 3rd edn N.Y., Macmillan. [**120**]

JAHODA, G. (1953) 'Social class attitudes and levels of occupational aspiration in secondary modern school leavers', *Br. J. Psych.*, **44**, 95–107. [**121**]

JAMES, I. P. (1966) 'The heroin problem,' *Medical News*, 16 Sept. [**122**]

JAMES, I. P. (1967) 'Suicide and mortality amongst heroin addicts in Britain', *Br. J. Addict.*, **62**, No. 1/2, 391–8. [**123**]

JAPANESE GOVERNMENT: Ministry of Health and Welfare (1968) Personal communication. [**124**]

KALDEGG, A. (1967) 'Heroin addiction', *New Society* 2 Feb. [**125**]

KALDEGG, A. (1968) 'A psychologist's approach to drug addiction', *Br. J. Addict.*, **63**, No. 1/2, 71–4. [**126**]

KELLMAN, M., BUTLER, N. and DAVIS, R. (1967) *11,000 Seven year olds*, Studies in Child Development, Routledge & Kegan Paul. [**127**]

KENT POST-GRADUATE MEDICAL FEDERATION (1966) Report on a conference on the Problems of the Young Drug Taker, 7 May, *Lancet*, 28 May. [**128**]

KISSEN, D. M. (1960) 'Psycho-social factors in cigarette smoking motivation', *The Med. Officer*, **104**, 365–72. [**129**]

KLEE, G. D. (1963) 'LSD25 and ego functions', *Arch. Gen. Psychiat.*, **8**, No. 5, 461–74. [**130**]

KNAPP, P. H. (1952) 'Amphetamine and addiction', *J. Nerv. Ment. Dis.*, **115**, 406–32. [**131**]

KOSVINER, A., MITCHESON, M. C., MYERS, K., OGBORNE, A., STIMSON, G. V., ZACUNE, J. and EDWARDS, G. (1968) 'Heroin use in a provincial town', *Lancet*, 1 June, 1189–92. [**132**]

KRUG, D. *et al.* (1965) 'Inhalation of commercial solvents', in Harms, op. cit. [**133**]

LASKI, M. (1961) *Ecstasy*, Crescent Press. [**134**]

LASKOWITZ, D. (1965) 'Psychological characteristics of the adolescent addict', in Harms, op. cit. [**135**]

LASKOWITZ, D. and EINSTEIN, S. (1965) 'Gaol behaviour of adolescent addicts and delinquents non-addicted peers', *Psychological Reports*, **17**, NO. 1, 102. [**136**]

LAURIE, P. (1967) *Drugs*, Penguin Books. [**137**]

LEECH, K. (1967) 'Danger on the drug scene', *Daily Telegraph*, 8 Dec. [**138**]

LEECH, K. and JORDAN, BRENDA (1967) *Drugs for Young People: their use and misuse*, Oxford. The Religious Education Press. [**139**]

LENDON, N. C. (1965) 'Drugs causing dependence', *Br. J. Addict.*, **61**, 115–24. [**140**]

LEVENDAL, L., MEZEL, A., NEMES, L. and MEZEI-ERDELY, E. (1967) 'Some data concerning the personality structure of alcoholic patients', *Br. J. Addict.*, **62**, No. 3/4, 317–30. [**141**]

LEWIN, L. (1964) *Phantastica: Narcotics and Stimulating Drugs,* Routledge & Kegan Paul (1st publ. Germany 1924). [**142**]

LICHTENSTEIN, P. (1966) 'Narcotic addiction', in O'Donnell and Ball, op. cit. [**143**]

LINDESMITH, A. (1966) 'Basic problems in the social psychology of addiction and a theory', in O'Donnell and Ball, op. cit. [**144**]

LING, T. and BUCKMAN, J. (1963) *Lysergic Acid (LSD25) and Ritalin in the Treatment of Neurosis*, Lamborde Press. [**145**]

LINKEN, A. (1968) 'A study into drug taking amongst young patients attending a clinic for venereal diseases', unpublished report. [**146**]

LINTON, H. R., LANGS, R. J. and PAUL, I. H. (1964) 'Retrospective alterations of the LSD25 experience', *J. Nerv. Ment. Dis.*, **138**, No. 5, 409–23. [**147**]

LONDON SCHOOL OF HYGIENE AND TROPICAL MEDICINE, Study Group of the Public Health Department (1959) 'The smoking habits of school children', *Br. J. of Preventive and Social Med.*, **13**, 1–4. [**148**]

LOURIA, D. (1966) *Nightmare Drugs*, New York, Pocket Book Inc. [**149**]

LOWRY, J. and SIMSELL, E. V. (1963) 'Medicine and Law in the treatment of drug addiction', *Bull. on Narcotics*, **15**, July–Dec. [**150**]

MACDONALD, L. (1965) ' "Psychopathology" of narcotic addiction', in Harms, op. cit. [**151**]

MCKELLAR, P. (1963) 'Mescalin in human thinking', in Delay, op. cit. [**152**]

MCKENNELL, A. C. and BYNNER, J. M. (1969) 'Self images and smoking behaviour among school boys', *Br. J. Ed. Psych.*, **39**, No. 1, 27–39. [**153**]

MALITZ, S. *et al.* (1962) 'Drug versus psychotic hallucinations', in WEST, L. J. *Hallucinations*, Grune & Stratton. [**154**]

Melody Maker (1967) 'Beatle Paul and LSD', 1 July. [155]

MONROE, J. and ALEXANDER, W. (1961) 'Identification processes in hospitalised narcotic drug addicts', *J. Abnorm. (soc.) Psychol.*, **63**, 215–18. [156]

MONTAGU, A. (1965) 'The long search for euphoria', in *Time/Life* Special Report, op. cit. [157]

MURPHY, H. B. M. (1963) 'The cannabis habit: a review of recent psychiatric literature', *Bull. on Narcotics*, **15**, Jan.–March, 1. [158]

MUSGROVE, F. (1964) *Youth and the Social Order,* Routledge & Kegan Paul. [159]

NEW YORK ACADEMY OF MEDICINE (1966) 'Report on drug addiction', in O'Donnell and Ball, op. cit. [160]

NYLANDER, I. (1965) ' "Thinner" addiction in Sweden', in Harms, op. cit. [161]

NYSWANDER, M. (1965) 'The withdrawal treatment of adolescent drug addicts', in Harms, op. cit. [162]

Observer Review (1967) 'Drugs', 12 Feb. [163]

O'DONNELL, J. A. and BALL, J. C. (1966) *Narcotic Addiction*, New York, Harper & Row. [164]

OGBORNE, A. (1968) 'Society at work: Among heroin users', *New Society*, 6 June. [165]

PALMAE, G., STOREY, P. B. and BRISCOE, D. (1967) 'Social class and the young offender', *Br. J. Psychiat*, **113**, 1073–82. [166]

PATRICIA, SISTER (1966) *Drugs and Young People*, London, The Mothers' Union. [167]

PATRICK, S. (1965) 'Institutional treatment of the juvenile narcotic user', in Harms, op. cit. [168]

RAISON, T. (1966) *Youth in Society*, Hart-Davis. [169]

RATHOD, N. H., ALARCON, R. DE and THOMSON, I. G. (1967) 'Signs of heroin usage detected by drug users and their parents', *Lancet*, 30 Dec. 1411–14. [170]

REED, F. S. (1964) Letter to the editor, *Br. Med. J.*, 8 April. [171]

REICHARD, J. D. (1946) 'Some myths about marijuana', *Federal Probation*, 4, 4. [172]

REISMAN, D. (1964) *Individualism Reconsidered*, New York, Free Press of Glencoe. [173]

RETTIG, S. and PARMANICK, B. (1964) 'Subcultural identification of hospitalised male addicts: A further examination', *J. Nerv. Ment. Dis.*, 1, 83–6. [174]

ROSENTHAL, E. *et al.* (1965) 'The development of narcotics addiction among the newborn', in Harms, op. cit. [175]

SANDISON, R. A. (1968) 'The hallucinogenic drugs', *Practitioner*, 200, 244–50. [176]

SCHER, J. (1966) 'Patterns and profiles of addiction and drug abuse', *Arch. Gen. Psychiat.*, 15, No. 5, 539–51. [177]

SCHOFIELD, M. (1965) *The Sexual Behaviour of Young People*, Longmans. [178]

SCHUR, E. M. (1962) *Narcotic Addiction in Britain and America*, Indiana Press. [179]

SCOTT, P. and WILLCOX, D. (1965) 'Delinquency and amphetamines', *Br. J. Addict.*, 61, No. 1/2, 9–27. [180]

SECORD, P. F. and BACKMAN, C. (1964) *Social Psychology*, New York, McGraw-Hill. [181]

SHARPLESS, S. K. (1965) 'Hypnotics and sedatives: 1, The Barbiturates', in Goodman, L. S. and Gilman, A. (eds.) *The Pharmacological basis of Therapeutics*, 3rd edn. New York, Macmillan. [182]

SHARPLEY, ANNE (1964) Article in the *Evening Standard*, 3/4 Feb. [183]

SHEPERD, M., LADER, M. and RODNIGHT, R. (1968) *Clinical Psychopharmacology*, London, English Universities Press. [184]

SILBERMAN, H. (1967) *Aspects of Drug Addiction*, The Royal London Prisoners Aid Society, July. [185]

STAFFORD, P. and GOLIGHTLY, B. (1967) *LSD the problem solving Psychedelic*, Tandem Publications, 1967. [186]

STEINBERG, H., RUSHTON, R. and TINSON, CHRISTINE (1961) 'Modification of the effects of an amphetamine-barbiturate mixture by the past experience of rats', *Nature*, 11 Nov., 4802, 533–5. [187]

STEWART, M. (1950) 'The leisure activities of grammar school children', *Br. J. Ed. Psychol.*, 20, 11–34. [188]

Sunday Times Magazine (1967) 'Our girl's vital statistics', May. [189]

TAYLOR, W. (1967) 'An analysis of the problems presented in the use of LSD', *Bulletin on Narcotics*, 19, 1. [190]

Time/Life Special Report (1965) *The Drug Takers*, New York, Time Inc. [191]

Times, The (1967) 'A dangerous press campaign' (editorial), 28 Feb. [192]

Times, The (1968) 'School drug-taking in country grows', 13 May. [193]

TROCCHI, A. (1966) *Cain's Book*, Calder. [194]

TYLDEN, ELIZABETH (1966) Letter to the editor, *Lancet*, 30 July. [195]

UNDERLEIDER, J. T. (1966) 'The dangers of LSD', *J.A.M.A.*, August, 389–92. [196]

UNITED STATES: President Kennedy's Advisory Commission on Narcotic and Drug Abuse (1963) *Final Report*, November. [197]

VENESS, T. (1962) *School Leavers*, Methuen. [198]

VOLKMAN, R. and CRESSY, D. (1963) 'Differential association and the rehabilitation of drug addicts', *Am. J. Sociol.*, 69, 129–42. [199]

WALLACE, G. B. (chairman) (1944) *The Marijuana Problem in the City of New York, Mayor's Committee on Marijuana*, Lancaster P.A., Jacques Cattell Press. [200]

WEECH, A. P. (1966) 'The narcotic addict and "the Street" ', *Arch. Gen. Psychiat.*, 14, 299–305. [201]

WEIL, A., ZINBERG, N. and NELSON, J. (1968) Clinical and psychological effects of marijuana in man', *Science*, 162, 13 Dec., 1234–42. [202]

WEST, D. J. (1967) *The Young Offender*, Penguin Books. [203]

WHITCHURCH HOSPITAL, CARDIFF (1964) Report of a conference on Teenage Drug Taking on 23 March 1964, *Br. Med. J.*, 8 April. [204]

WILKINS, L. T. (1964) *Social Deviance*, Tavistock. [205]

WILKINS, L. T. (1965) 'A behavioural theory of drug taking', *Howard J. of Penology and Crime Prevention*, 11, 4. [206]

WILLIS, J. H. (1966) 'Heroin addiction in young people', *Guy's Hospital Gazette*, 5 March. [207]

WILLIS, J. H. (1968) 'Some problems of opiate addiction', *Practitioner*, 200, 220–5. [208]

WILSON, C. W. M. and LINKEN, A. (1967) 'The use of cannabis in relation to the adolescent', unpublished paper. [209]

WILSON-KAY, B. (1967) Personal communication. [210]

WINICK, C. (1965) 'Marijuana use by young people', in Harms, op. cit. [211]

WOOD, A. J. (1967) *Drug Dependence*, Corp. of Bristol and the British Council of Social Services. [212]

WORLD HEALTH ORGANISATION (1964) Report Series No. 273 on addiction producing drugs, 13th Report, W.H.O. Geneva. [213]

WORLD HEALTH ORGANISATION (1964) Report Series No. 287. W.H.O. expert committee; Evaluation of dependence-producing drugs, Geneva. [214]

WORLD HEALTH ORGANISATION (1966) Report Series No. 343. W.H.O. expert committee on dependence producing drugs, 15th Report, Geneva. [215]

WRIGHT, J. D. (1968) 'A survey of the knowledge and attitudes about drug misuse among 4th year pupils at three Wolverhampton schools', *Health Ed. J.*, 27, No. 3, 111–14. [216]

ZACUNE, J., MITCHESON, M. and MALONE, S. (1969) 'Heroin use in a provincial town—One year later', unpublished report. [217]

2. METHODOLOGY

EDWARDS, A. L. (1957) *Techniques of Attitude Scale Construction*, New York, Appleton-Century-Crofts. [218]

HARMAN, H. (1965) *Modern Factor Analysis*, University of Chicago Press. [219]

HENDRIKSON, A. E. and WHITE, P. C. (1964) 'Promax: a quick method for rotation to oblique simple structure', *Br. J. Statist. Psychol.*, **17**, 65–70. [220]

JAHODA, M., DEUTSCH, M. and COOK, S. W. (1952) *Research methods in Social Relations: Part 1: Basic Processes*, Dryden Press. [221]

KAUSER, J. F. (1958) 'The varimax criterion for analytical rotation in factor analysis', *Psychmetrike*, **23**, 187–200. [222]

KINSEY, A. (1948) *Sexual Behaviour in the Human Male*, Philadelphia, Saunders. [223]

OPPENHEIM, A. N. (1966) *Questionnaire Design and Attitude Measurement*, Heinemann Educational Books. [224]

SIEGEL, S. (1956) *Nonparametric Statistics for the Behavioural Sciences*, McGraw-Hill. [225]

3. ATTITUDE CHANGE

COHEN, A. (1964) *Attitude Change and Social Influence*, Basic Books [226]

HARE, A. P. (1962) *Handbook of Small Group Research*, Free Press. [227]

HOVLAND, C. I. (1960) *The Order of Presentation in Persuasion*, Yale University Press [228]

JANIS, I and HOVLAND, C. (1959) *Personality and Persuasion*, Yale University Press. [229]

JANIS, I. and TERWILLIDGER, R. (1962) 'An experimental study of psychological resistances to fear arousing communications', *J. Abnorm. (soc.) Psychol.*, **65**, 403–10. [230]

KATZ, E. and LAZARSFELD, P. (1964) *Personal influence*, Free Press. [231]

KRECH, I., CRUTCHFIELD, R. et al. (1962) *Individual in Society*, McGraw-Hill. [232]

LEVENTHAL, L. and WATTS, J. C. (1966) 'Sources of resistance to fear-arousing communications on smoking and lung cancer', *J. Person.*, **34**, 155–75. [233]

ROSENBERG, M. J. (1960) *Attitude Change and Organization*, Yale University Press. [234]

SCHRAMM, W. (1963) *The Science of Human Communication*, Basic Books. [235]

Index